# RYA Crew to Win

Written by Joe Glanfield


First Published 2006

The Royal Yachting Association
RYA House, Ensign Way
Hamble, Southampton
Hampshire SO31 4YA

Tel: 0845 345 0400
Fax: 0845 345 0329
E-mail: publications@rya.org.uk
Web: www.rya.org.uk

ISBN 1905104200 RYA Order Code G39

## Acknowledgements

I would firstly like give a huge thank you to both Nick Rogers and Steve Morrison for helming the boats and giving advice. My sponsors, Volvo Cars, UK Sport, Holt Fittings and North Sails.

Finally I would like to give special thanks to David Cole for his help in our Olympic sailing.

## Photo Credits

Forecast chart Alistar Garrald, RS. Sailboats, 49er Class Association, 29er Class Association, 420 Class Association, Neill Blume, Peter Bentley and a big thank you to Richard Langdon of OceanImages.

A CIP record of this book is available from the British Library.

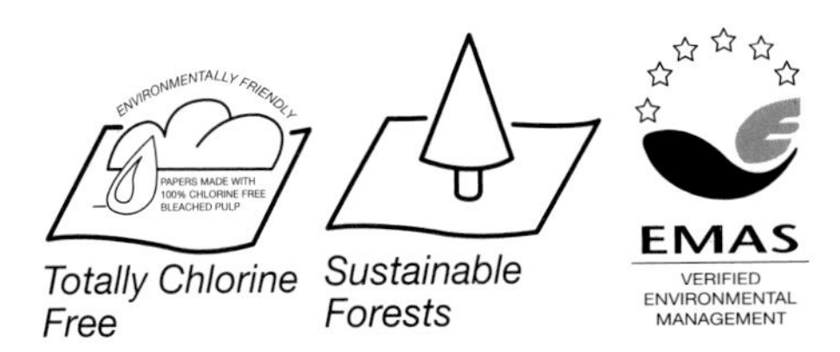


Published by **The Royal Yachting Association**
RYA House, Ensign Way, Hamble, Southampton SO31 4YA
**Tel:** 0845 345 0400
**Fax:** 0845 345 0329
**Email:** publications@rya.org.uk
**Web:** www.rya.org.uk





**Cover design:** Pete Galvin
**Typeset:** Batt Creative
**Text Editor:** Chris Harris
**Technical Editor:** Alan (Spod) Olive
**Proof-reading and indexing:** Alan Thatcher
**Printed by:** Printed in Malta by Gutenberg Press
Ring 0845 345 0400 for a free copy of our Publications Catalogue.

# Contents

# Contents

# Contents

# Contents



Throughout the book you will see references to: **See Training Exercises**
All these exercises are in Chapter 17.

# Foreword

For many people, crews are seen as a necessary evil - someone to blame when they don't win - and as for recognition - it's only the guy on the tiller that counts.

Crew to Win explodes the myth that helms and crew are different - that they can do their tasks independently and hope to be successful. The team is a vital ingredient to any crewed boats' success and the saying that "the whole is greater than the sum of the parts" is a truism in our sport - if you want to be truly successful.

What makes this book so great is that it's written by one of GBR's top dinghy crews, who I first met in 1996, soon after he teamed up with Nick Rogers in the 470. They qualified and finished 4th in the 2000 Olympic Games in Sydney - and were devastated. However, they went on to win Silver in Athens in 2004 and are continuing to campaign, winning the 470 European Championships again in 2005. The fact that their partnership is still so strong is a testament to the respect the team shares and the terrific skills Joe possesses as crew in that team.

More recently, Joe is proving to be an inspirational coach, able to articulate his approach to help future generations of sailors and this book allows readers an insight into the process of successful crewing.

This book is a must have for crews and helms who aspire to success.

**John Derbyshire**

Manager/Performance Director RYA Racing

# Introduction

Throughout my sailing career I have been continually surprised how quickly improvements can be made. I will never forget watching the Olympics in 1996 as a sixteen year old and thinking how much I would love to be able to compete at that level. I didn't believe for a second that I would be there in four years' time racing for a medal.

I have always maintained that most of my initial success in sailing was due to the fact I simply sailed more then anyone else. Between the ages of 13-16 years old there was a group of us at my local sailing club, 'Exe,' that spent all our free time sailing and when we weren't sailing we were either talking or thinking about it. This is simply because it was what we loved to do, our friends were there and the people around us made it enjoyable. Still, after eight years of sailing fulltime there is nothing I enjoy more than to get in a boat and compete in a race.

Sailing a double-handed boat is ultimately about the team rather then the helm or the crew and I was very lucky to team up with Nick Rogers when I started Olympic sailing, finally I had met someone who was even more passionate about the Olympics than me and, not to mention very good at making a boat go fast (especially whilst under the pressure of a big race). What was most interesting when I first started sailing with Nick was that despite achieving very similar things at youth level, we approached sailing in a very different way and our strengths and weaknesses were nearly opposites. Due to the confidence we had in our own ability and each others' we were able to be open to each others' views and design a way of communicating that heavily played on each others' strengths whilst blanketing our individual weaknesses.

It has been a very enjoyable challenge writing this book and deciding what to include and how best to explain the various topics. I wanted this book to be as practical as possible, so sailors could use the information to directly improve their sailing ability. In the past I have read books stuffed full of technical jargon that sound very complicated but were dull to read and hard to translate to the water; this is what I was desperate to avoid. There is no denying that sailing is a technical sport with a huge number of variables, but the best way to deal with this is to break it down, prioritize and first of all become very good at the basics.

I have always believed that in a sport like sailing there is plenty of room for individual personality and all successful teams have very clear ideas about how they approach training and competition and how to generate the best performance from themselves. I hope through reading this book my approach and attitude will come across to you as ultimately this is as important as the individual skills.

Enjoy the book, and I hope it helps bring success to your racing, remember, 'things don't come to those who wait', get training.

**Joe Glanfield**

ROGERS
GLANFIELD

# 1 Getting Started

## Helm or Crew?

The decision to helm or crew should not have to be a permanent one. If you learn to do both it will help you become a more rounded sailor, and will also help with your team work as you will understand your team-mates' jobs and be better equipped to discuss ways to move forward in your training.

I originally started helming and switched to crewing primarily because of my size, but also because being part of a good partnership was more important to me than the role I played. I knew someone at my sailing club who was also a helm. We both wanted to sail the same type of boat, we had a similar level of commitment and had complementary skills. It made more sense for us to team up, and for one of us to switch to crewing than for both to look for crews who might be less compatible. I enjoyed crewing more than my friend and was the better size, so I made the switch.

### Things that will affect the Helm or Crew decision:

- Personal preference.
- The class of boat you want to sail.
- Your size compared to the optimum size for the role.
- Will one role let you use your sailing strengths more than the other?
- The availability and suitability of other sailors.

You will need to consider many things when deciding whether to helm or crew, but from my experience the most important is the person you are considering sailing with. If you know someone you think would make a good team-mate for you, it is usually worth trying to make it work, even if one of you has to switch from their normal role.

## Choosing the Class of Boat

There are numerous different classes of boat to choose from, all offering different things to the sailor. Before you commit to buying a certain type of boat it is worth getting as many details as possible. All classes have different size and weight requirements, fleet sizes and standards of racing. Some classes will be more challenging to sail around a course and so require a lot of time working on boat-handling. Others may be quite easy to sail in most conditions and consequently need a high emphasis on tactics if you are to be successful. A good starting point is to have a look at what classes are popular at your local sailing club. By sailing one of these classes you can often get good advice, and there is usually lots of second-hand kit available.

### Things to consider when choosing a class

- The ideal weight and size of the class.
- The size of the national fleet.
- The standard of racing.
- How difficult the boat is to handle
- If the class has international events.
- If it is one design or a development class.
- The social programme.
- If the class is growing or shrinking nationally.

If you are a youth sailor it is worth looking at the RYA-recognized classes as they offer good, organized racing and will have regular training weekends aimed at different standards.

The Olympic classes offer something completely different and are not recommended for beginners. It is possible to race in these classes without doing an Olympic campaign (which requires a very high level of commitment), but the standard is very advanced and the approach more serious than in other national classes. Most Olympic sailors are full-time, but there are also a number of part-time sailors who have got to the front of national classes and who want the challenge of Olympic-standard racing.

49er

29er

420

RS400

# 2 Creating a Winning Team

Finding the right person to sail with is not easy. It is made more difficult by the fact the sport is so vast in terms of what an individual can get out of it. Some people want to go for a picnic and a trip around the bay once a month whereas others in the same club have aspirations of sailing full-time and going to the Olympics. I believe a team, and in particular a partnership, needs to work in a way that utilizes the skills of the individuals in order to reach its full potential.

It is important to have your own goals and ambitions clearly mapped out before approaching someone to sail with; this will help any potential team-mate decide if they are interested in what you are proposing. Before you even set foot in a boat it is worth asking each other some fundamental questions.

It is unlikely that you will be in agreement over all these issues and some are more important than others, but compromises might need to be made in order to avoid problems later on.

Once you have formed your partnership it is a good idea to divide the onshore responsibilities. In our team Nick (Rogers) takes care of the boat work and making sure we have up-to-date spares. I make sure all our travel arrangements and funding are organized. For media and sponsors we share the jobs and try to attend things together to make sure we present a united front. Obviously there are significantly less logistics for a club sailor than for an Olympic campaign, but by dividing the jobs you should be able to hit the water with no gear failure, with forecast, tide and course checked, and sandwiches and flask ready.

### Considerations for potential team-mates

- Is your combined size right for the boat you want to sail?
- How much sailing do you want to do?
- If you work, how much holiday are you willing to put towards sailing?
- Where are you going to sail?
- Are you going to sail during the winter?
- How much money are you willing to invest in your sailing?
- How highly do you prioritize sailing among other hobbies and interests?
- Are your sailing skills complementary?
- Do you respect what the other person has to offer?
- Could you get on with each other socially?

GBR
NED
GBR

# 2 Creating a Winning Team

## Training in a New Team

If possible, try to make your first sail in a new team away from competition and other boats. Make it as fun as possible and just get a feel for how the other person sails. When you start in a new team it is the communication and roles in the boat that will need work and clarification. Once you feel ready, try sailing around a windward-to-leeward course big enough for you to discuss ideas in between mark-roundings and manoeuvres. When you are confident that your processes in the boat are established, shorten the course. You can do this as much as is comfortable for you; the shorter you make it, the more hectic it will feel and the better insight you will get into your team's readiness (or lack of it) for the pressures of a real race. Remember, as a team, you will be on a steep learning curve at this stage so it is worth investing as much time on the water as possible so the momentum is not broken. Once the processes feel natural you can back off.

### Golden rules for teamwork

- Respect each other's opinion.
- Trust that the other is doing their utmost to achieve the team's common goal.
- Accept differences in approach and make room for individual flair.
- Once you commit to a decision, support each other and pursue it whole-heartedly.
- Appreciate that there will be disagreements.
- Play to each other's strengths on and off the water, even if it means going out of your way to help with something they struggle to do.
- Always conceal any weaknesses or problems within the team from your competitors.

## Team Attitude

In order to get the most from crewing it is essential that you and your team-mate accept that, by sailing a double-handed (or more) dinghy, you are competing in a team sport, and that you cannot achieve your goals without the other team member(s). As with all relationships, your attitude and the effort you are willing to put into your team will make a big difference to its success. Above are some golden rules that work for the teams I am involved with:

# 3 Dinghy Sailing Clothing and Equipment

The sailing clothing you will need depends very much on what time of the year you intend to go sailing. Whether you wear a wetsuit or drysuit, you want it to be hard-wearing, lightweight (in most cases) and allow good freedom of movement. Here are some things to consider before:

### Buying a Wetsuit

- Bear in mind you will be wearing it sometimes when there is a minimal amount of spray, so it needs to be comfortable when dry.
- Avoid smooth skin material as it rips easily and tends to grip to things on the boat.
- Make sure the neck allows you good freedom of movement so you can look around easily.
- The wetsuit needs to be comfortable when bending both your elbows and knees, so look for one with more flexible material in these areas.
- Most high-performance boat crews prefer Long John (sleeveless) wetsuits as they do not restrict arm and shoulder movements.

### Buying a Drysuit

- Choose whether you want a breathable or standard drysuit. Breathable material tends to be softer and more comfortable, but it is important to remember the breathable qualities will only work if all your other layers are breathable, including what you wear on top.
- Drysuits are available with a zip across the front or the shoulders. A zip across the shoulders is more comfortable while sailing, especially if wearing a trapeze harness, but harder to get out of.
- Find a suit that is as tight-fitting as possible while still allowing you to stretch and crouch comfortably.

## Buoyancy Aid

The buoyancy aid should be the correct size for the sailor's height and weight, tight-fitting and with as few buckles as possible. It should have the British Kitemark label which confirms it is an approved make and design. A common mistake is to buy buoyancy aids too big, especially when buying for growing children. The temptation is to think being bigger means the buoyancy aid will give the sailor even more buoyancy but actually it will ride up under the sailor's arms, making it harder to swim when in the water, and is more likely to fall off.

## Trapeze Harness

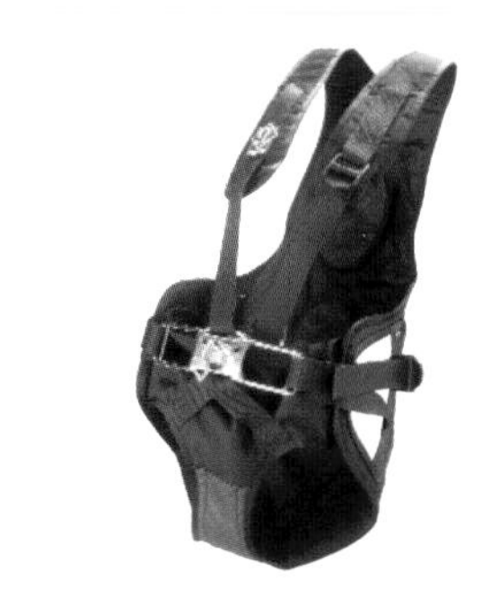

A trapeze harness needs to be a comfortable fit around the hips and in the lower back. It should have straps over the shoulders and adjusters across the hips to keep the hook close to your body. Under the International Sailing Federation rules the harness must give positive buoyancy and be within the class's weight restrictions.

## Footwear

It is important to have footwear with a thin, bendy sole and good grip, particularly if you are trapezing. Make sure the boot is tight around the heel and have either elastic or a strap, otherwise it could easily fall off if it gets caught on something. Remember that if you intend to wear a drysuit with socks you will need a bigger boot size.

## Hiking Shorts

Hiking shorts definitely make it more comfortable and easier to hike for long periods of time. The best hiking shorts have straps over the shoulders so they don't slip around. They usually are part of a three quarter length wetsuit short, meaning you have knee pads and the edge of the hiking shorts won't rub in the crease of your knee. Be wary of hiking shorts that are mostly straps and go over your kit, they are light but also difficult to get a good fit and the buckles can get caught on things on the boat.

## Other Equipment

It is a good idea to wear a tight rash top over the top of all your sailing kit, especially if you are sailing a fast high-performance boat. It reduces windage and keeps your buoyancy aid and harness tucked away and tidy.

When choosing a start-timer make sure it has got a large, clear display, and if you intend wearing it on your wrist a good strong strap. It is usually best to have the numbers on the front rather than the side.

# 4 Fitness for Sailing

The physical demands of sailing will vary from class to class, and most sailors are unaware of how much their fitness affects their technique and decision-making. In most sports it is obvious when your fitness is not up to the job, but in sailing poor fitness can easily be attributed to other things such as equipment or simply being unlucky. You need to think whether your fitness prevents you sailing the boat to the best of your ability in every condition from day one until the end of the regatta.

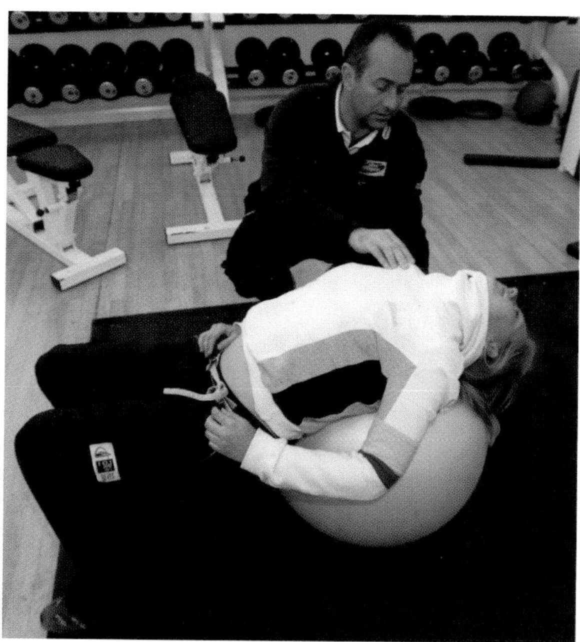

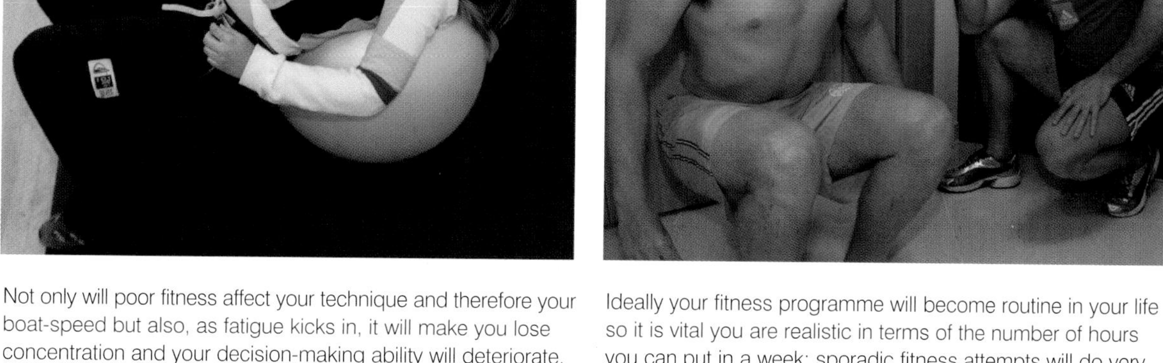

Not only will poor fitness affect your technique and therefore your boat-speed but also, as fatigue kicks in, it will make you lose concentration and your decision-making ability will deteriorate.

It is important to be as organized with your fitness programme as you are with your sailing. Set yourself a programme and goals that cover all of the areas set out .

### Things to consider in your fitness programme

- Diet.
- Weight.
- Aerobic fitness.
- Anaerobic fitness.
- Core stability.
- Flexibility.

Ideally your fitness programme will become routine in your life so it is vital you are realistic in terms of the number of hours you can put in a week; sporadic fitness attempts will do very little for your fitness but will increase your chance of injury.

Keeping up a high number of hours on the water is also crucial for your sailing fitness because a lot of the movements in the boat are hard to replicate onshore. Even if you have been doing a lot of onshore work you can still come in off the water aching if you have not been sailing for a while.

# 5 Goal Setting

The ability to set and monitor your goals is essential in sport, especially in a sport with as many variables as sailing. There are many ways to use goal setting to help with your training and progress. I believe, in general, people make goal setting too complicated so that it is impractical to use and update regularly. It is a good idea to get a coach or someone who knows your sailing well to help you with your goal setting. Everything should be written down and kept for future reference.

## Dream Goal

It is worth first of all having a think about what you ideally want to achieve in sailing. This can be something that is not likely to happen for a long time. At the time when you write the goal down it might look unrealistic, but it will help you define what your more immediate outcome goals are and then, hopefully, in the future it will become an outcome goal in itself.

## Outcome Goals

The next thing to do is write down your outcome goal. I think you should only have one main outcome goal per season even though there is likely to be more than one event where you want to get a good result (these extra events can be process goals towards the outcome goal). Having one goal will help with visualization, which in turn helps you to peak at the right time.

## Process Goals

Sailors will often use the dartboard diagram (page 22) to map out their process goals. The goal must be SMART (specific, measurable, attainable, realistic and time-based) because all your process goals, which dictate your training, will stem from this goal. A common mistake, though, is not to use it in conjunction with the outcome goal, without which the scores have little relevance. If you take a score of 10 as where you need to be to attain your outcome goal it gives you a way to measure how much work you have to do in each highlighted area. For example, you might not be very good at light-wind tacks, but you know the venue of your outcome goal is unlikely to have light winds, so although you are only a 6 in terms of ability, it is good enough for your outcome goal, therefore a 10. The aspect of your sailing that you choose to put in each segment is up to you. You could have one dartboard with general areas and another with more specific details of one of the highlighted areas. Once you have highlighted the areas of concern, write down ideas on how you can improve. This will give direction to your training days because you will know what you want to get out of each day. It will also help you decide how much training to do and how many events to attend. You will probably find that, at first, your process goals are not very detailed, but once you start training in that aspect you are able to amend them and make the process goals more specific.

## Monitoring Training Sessions

Once you have highlighted your process goals, it is essential to keep monitoring them. Each time you go sailing fill in a training-day sheet (see page 24) that specifies what you wanted to achieve, how you were going to do it, what you did achieve, and what to do next time you get similar conditions. You will find the notes useful in committing things to memory and it will prevent you from being distracted into other areas.

Each month, do a review of your training and fill in another dartboard diagram (see page 22) to check on your progress with your process goals. If you have not improved in certain areas, have a look through your training-day sheets and see if you have neglected those areas or have not been doing the correct exercises. This is likely to instigate more goal setting and stimulate ideas on how to move closer to achieving the outcome goal.

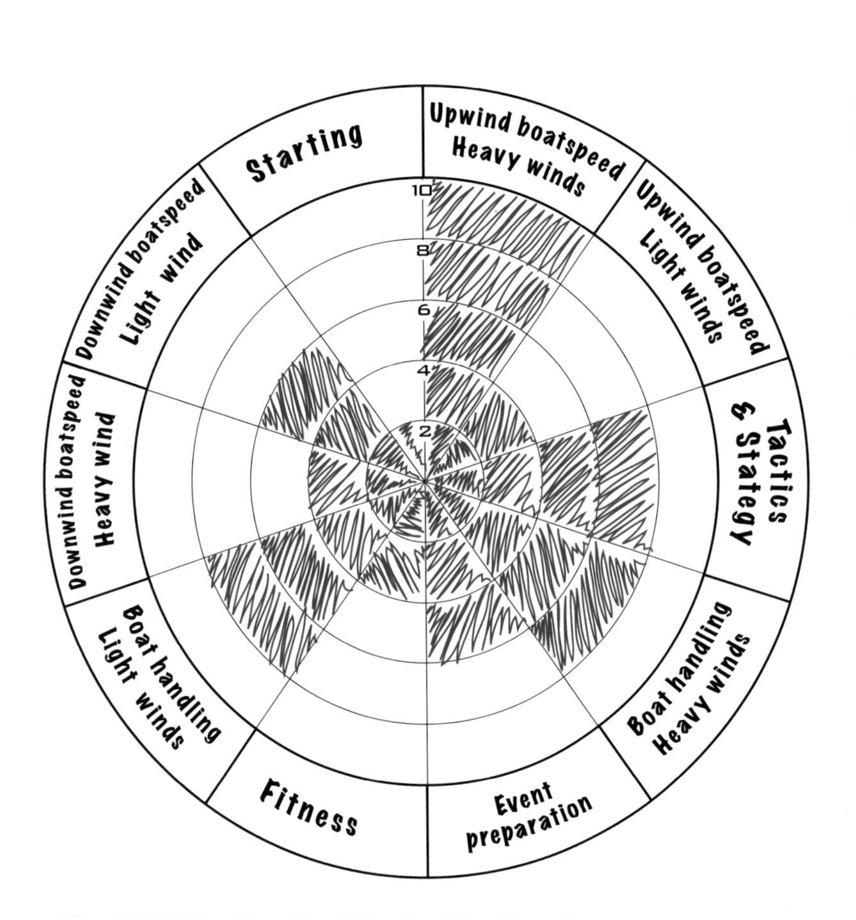


## General Evaluation

This dartboard shows that the area of 'starting' needs the most work to achieve the outcome goal, whilst 'Upwind boat speed in heavy winds' needs the least amount of work.

## Area of Specific Evaluation - Starting

This dartboard takes a closer look at areas of starting and shows that training should be focused on acceleration and light wind starting.

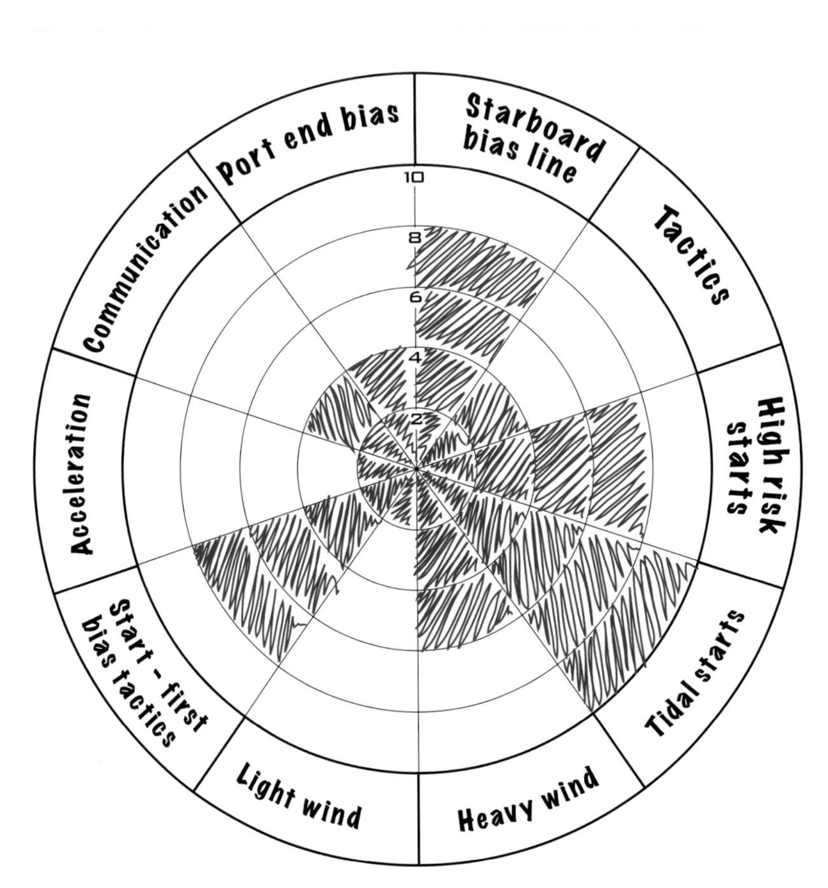

## Example Goal Setting Sheet

Dream Goal: Win class world championships

Outcome Goal: Top 10 National Championships

Date: August this year

Sailing days till outcome goal (approx): 28 days

Process goals:

1. Improve light wind starting
2. Improve strong wind downwind technique
3. Lose 5kg weight
4. Gain event experience

Action plan:

Find other sailors to train with and practise tight congested mock starts working on acceleration and communication when the wind is light.

In strong winds sail long downwind tuning legs with training partner, try and get a coach to look at our technique and take some video for us.

Improve diet, no pudding after supper. Increase aerobic fitness sessions from two sessions to four per week.

Attend two extra open meetings before nationals with the goal of finishing in the top ten in both.

### Example Day Training Sheet

Date: 1st April this year

Venue: Weymouth Bay

Conditions: Building southwesterly sea breeze started 5 knots and built to 12 knots, sea state was a small, short chop.

Length of sail: 3 hours

Goals for training session: Work on acceleration by doing 5 short line practice starts concentrating on timing between helm and crew. Lengthen line and start in the middle on a transit for 3 starts working on judging approach to transit. Finish off with 2 short practice races to put the starting into the context of a race.

Training review: Launched slightly late, completed 5 short line starts. They were much better at starboard end compared to port. The transit starts exercise was not very worthwhile, as we needed someone to look at the end of the line to judge our accuracy. On the first race we made a good start but went the wrong way up the first beat. The second race was better starting at the starboard end and tacking to the right of the beat leading at the windward mark. Our hoists were useless though and we lost the lead.

Ideas for future training (new process goals): We need to work for longer on port bias lines. We also need to do more short races so we have to match up the start with the first beat tactics. Our hoists were poor and need more work to improve speed.

**Example Monthly Report Sheet**

Month: April this year

No of hours sailing per condition:
0-5 knots - 0 hours    6-10 knots - 6 hours
11-15 knots - 8 hours    16-20 knots - 4 hours
21+ knots - 0 hours
Events completed: Exe open meeting, finished 11th, goal 10th

Length of sail: 3 hours

Improvements in process goals Light wind starting improved from 4-6 on dartboard. Strong wind downwind, no improvement. Lost 2kg of weight, so on target. Finished 11th at open meeting outside of target but learnt a lot.

Goals for next month (process goals): We need to spend more time in extreme light and strong conditions. Target long downwind legs in 15+knots trainings. Achieve top 10 at next open meeting. Continue with diet and fitness programme.

**Dream Goal**

Dream Goal:

Outcome Goal:

Date:

Sailing days till outcome goal (approx):

Process goals:

Action plan:

**Outcome Goal**

Dream Goal:

Outcome Goal:

Date:

Sailing days till outcome goal (approx):

Process goals:

Action plan:

# 6 Boat Balance, Hiking and Trapezing

**HIKING**

Good technique for hiking is absolutely essential, not just for boat speed, but also to avoid injury. Your toe-straps should be adjusted to suit your leg length. If they are too long you will not be able to keep your legs straight; if too short you will end up compensating by throwing your upper body further backwards (or will just not get out far enough).

When you are maximum-hiked the gunwale should be approximately halfway down your thigh (slightly further out if you are fitter). You need to adopt a position you can hold for the entire race, trying to keep your legs and back as horizontal as possible. Not only does straight-leg hiking give you maximum leverage, it also puts you in a better position to look around the racecourse and makes it easier for the helmsman to sail the boat flat without your behind dragging.

See Training Exercise 1 & 3

### Basic Boat Balance

- Windward heel will make the boat want to bear away.
- Leeward heel will make the boat want to head up.
- There are other factors that affect boat balance, including rig and sail settings, fore and aft trim, and centreboard position.
- While sailing upwind the boat should be as flat as possible.
- Below maximum power (before the sails need to be eased) the boat balance is the crew's responsibility. Once above maximum power the helm will control the balance by easing the mainsail.

## Anticipation

Sailors often associate good boat balance with quick crew movements and, while this helps, good boat balance is really about anticipating changes in wind and sea state that will require adjustment before they hit. This reduces the need for quick, sudden crew movements and to achieve it you will need close communication between the helm and crew.

For more about downwind boat balance, see Chapter 11, Downwind Technique.

## Light Winds (Pre-Trapezing)

There are a number of ways to position yourself in the boat before you are needed on the side to hike or trapeze. Some crews sit on the floor of the boat facing backwards. The good thing about this technique is that it keeps your body weight low and far forward. Personally I don't like this technique as it means you can't play any part in the upwind tactics and it takes a big movement to adjust for small changes in wind or sea state. I prefer instead to sit across the boat with my legs to leeward, which means I can still see forward and adjust my upper body to windward or leeward as it is needed.

In high-performance boats the crews move up into a crouched position in front of the mast in light winds. Remember, no matter what boat you sail, it is vital that you keep your body away from the jib slot (the gap between the mainsail and jib), because the disturbance caused by blocking the slot will make the boat very slow.

*By lying across the boat when sat in I can stay forwards without my knees getting away and still keep my eyes on the wind. From here it is a smooth, swift movement outboard when a gust comes.*

*In a high performance boat you will need to get a long way forward in light winds, here I am playing the mainsail and remain on my feet so I can respond quickly to a gust.*

# 6 Boat Balance, Hiking and Trapezing

## Basic Trapezing Techniques

It is important to remember that, when you are trapezing, you are directly attached to the rig so, while using the trapeze to balance the boat you have to move as smoothly as possible because every movement could disturb the sails.

To move out onto the trapeze you hold the handle with the hand closest to the bow, then put your front leg onto the gunwale of the boat and push out, bringing your other leg out onto the gunwale. Once out, use your aft hand (which should be holding the jib sheet) to clip yourself on.

*The closer you can keep your feet toand stay on your toes the more leverage you will gain, but don't risk falling over!*

The process of moving in off the trapeze is nearly the same as moving out but in reverse. You take the handle with your front hand and take your body weight on that arm. Depending on your trapeze harness and hook, if you then lift your hips it will unhook you from the trapeze; if not, then simply use your other hand to unhook. You then bring your aft leg into the boat, first bending your front leg as you move in.

The reason to trapeze is to give more leverage to help balance the boat. Once on the trapeze you can use the adjustable trapeze lines to move yourself higher or lower depending on the wind strength. Remember there are many other ways you can increase the amount of leverage you are exerting. As well as lowering the trapeze lines, you can put your legs closer together and move onto tiptoes, you can straighten your legs and back and even put one or both hands behind your head. It is important to be able to use this full range of movement in order to move swiftly from marginal trapezing to flat trapezing and vice versa.

*Constantly feel the balance of the boat when moving out onto the trapeze and change your technique to keep the boat flat.*

# 6 Boat Balance, Hiking and Trapezing

## Advanced Trapezing Techniques

### FLAT TRAPEZING

Flat trapezing is the term used when there is enough wind to provide sufficient power in the rig for you to remain flat and straight on the trapeze. Once in these conditions it is the helm's responsibility to produce the correct amount of windward and leeward heel using the mainsheet, and as a crew it is vital you exert as much leverage as possible. Other than for the odd rogue wave you only move in if the wind has dropped enough for the helm to bring the boom in onto the centreline. Remember, when you are looking around for laylines or other information for tactical decisions, to be as quick as possible; every time you bend your back the rig is effectively losing power.

*Anticipating changes in wind speed and sea state is the key to good boat balance.*

### FORE AND AFT BOAT TRIM

Where you stand in the boat needs to be adjusted according to the conditions. When the boat is in displacement mode (not planing) you need to make sure you are standing far enough forward to provide full waterline length without digging the bow in. As the wind increases the boat will want to plane (the stage at which this happens depends on the type of boat you sail). At this point you need to move backwards in the boat so the bow can lift. If you are standing too far forward you will find it produces weather helm and makes the boat hard to bear away and go fast forward, but if you are standing too far back the boat will struggle to point high as there will be lee helm and the bow will be getting blown off the wind. In choppy, marginal trapezing conditions when you have to stand further back to stop the bow digging in, you might have to compensate for this by giving a tiny amount of leeward heel to avoid lee helm.

*When the wind is steady pull yourself as high as possible on your trapeze wire, this will dampen down your movements, making it easier to make subtle changes to the balance.*

*In gusty conditions lower yourself slightly bending your legs a bit more, this will allow you to make quicker differences to your leverage during changes in wind speed.*

## MARGINAL TRAPEZING

The most difficult trapezing is when the mainsail is on the centreline and there is not enough wind to flat-trapeze. In these conditions it is entirely your responsibility to keep the boat flat and balanced. If you bring the boat to windward it will want to bear away and if you let it heel to leeward it will want to point up.

As a crew it is important to change your technique according to the conditions. When sailing in choppy, steady wind conditions, you move to the highest point on your trapeze adjusters so you are almost standing on the side. This will damp down your body movements so that when you move it will make finer adjustments to your leverage to let you react to the subtle changes in wind pressure. When sailing in flatter water and more gusty conditions you need to leave yourself slightly lower on the trapeze and bend your legs further, keeping your back quite horizontal, so that when you move it will make big differences to your leverage. This is good for big gusts and lulls.

# 7 Tacking

## See Training Exercises 6 & 8

## Light-Wind Tacking

Just before the helm points up to tack, the boat needs to be allowed to heel slightly to leeward, reducing the amount of tiller needed to be used, which will cause less drag. At what point you roll the boat, and how much, depends on the wind strength, sea state and class of boat. In general it is best to start rolling the boat to windward (off the old tack) as the luff of the jib starts to back. This should happen later the less wind there is, as the tack will be slower, and you can afford to be later onto the new windward side after the tack. The helm's and crew's movements should be synchronized for the roll and across the boat. As a crew you need to judge by the wind strength how much help the helm will need to bring the boat flat on the new tack. It is important while tacking in light winds to remain as far forward as possible in the boat at all times.

In light winds the jib can afford to be backed for a split-second to help the bow around (and should not flap at all) before being pulled in on the new tack. Ideally the jib should be left eased a couple of inches from its normal set position, then pulled in the last bit as the boat is brought flat.

1

2

3

4

5

# 7 Tacking

## Wire to Wire Tacking

Your tacking technique in medium conditions will depend heavily on the type of boat you sail and the sea state. Your trapezing ability will be relied on to make the tack fast and smooth, as you need to remain out on the windward side as long as possible before the tack and then move across the boat and out onto the new side and onto the trapeze (see Basic Trapezing Techniques in Chapter 6) to pull the boat flat. It is important to unclip yourself and hold yourself on the handle before the helm starts steering into the tack; this will reduce the chance of remaining stuck on your hook as the boat goes head-to-wind. When holding onto the handle, keep a straight arm if the boat is overpowered, therefore keeping maximum leverage as the boat heads up.

1

1

When you move through the boat, keep your footsteps to a minimum. This is easier to repeat, and will make you faster through the boat and less likely to get caught up. As you move out on the trapeze, again keep a straight arm if the boat is overpowered, and bring the loop out to your hook when you clip on. In a medium-wind tack, as in a light-wind tack, you are still looking to try to let the jib back momentarily before pulling it in on the new side. To do this you will need to wait until you are inside the boat before uncleating the jib. This will take quite a lot of practice and getting it wrong can easily lead to a capsize.

I always tidy the jib sheet before I go into the tack and then I actually let go of it so I can only pick it up and uncleat it when I am moving across the boat.

## Heavy-Wind Tacking

Heavy-wind tacking uses nearly the same technique as a wire to wire tack, except there is a need to make the whole process safer. Remember, in strong winds you should not be tacking too often because of the amount of distance you lose each time you do it, the priority is to avoid any problems while you tack. It is normally best to uncleat the jib while out on the trapeze before the tack has started. You can then let it out as you come in for the tack. There are likely to be waves in heavy winds, so make sure you have a fairly wide stance on the trapeze as you go into the tack, to prevent yourself from being knocked off balance. Once on the new side, be quick to move back in the boat and at maximum leverage.

2

WWW.VOLVOCARS.CO.UK/SAILING

3

WWW.VOLVOCARS.CO.UK/SAILING

4

TEAM
VOLVO

5

TEAM
VOLVO

6

# 8 Sail Settings

## See Training Exercise 3

## Setting the Jib

The controls available to you and how you use them to correctly set your jib up will vary according to the type of boat you sail. It is important to remember that when you adjust one of the controls it will have an effect on the others. For this reason it is very important to have everything possible calibrated and clearly marked. When marking ropes, use small whippings rather than permanent marker; it is clearer and won't rub off.

## Rig Tension

How much rig tension you use will have a huge effect on the shape of the jib. If you pull more tension on, it will give a finer entry to the jib and move the draught (maximum depth) of the sail back; if you ease the rig tension it will increase the depth of the jib and move the draught forward. In all but the rarest of conditions I think it best not to adjust the rig tension too much from your standard setting because, while it will change the jib shape, it will also change a lot of other things, including the mainsail shape, mast rake and jib slot.

### Tools to calibrate the jib

- Telltales on jib and luff of mainsail.
- Jib sheet marks and calibration strip on boat next to mark.
- Spreader marks an inch apart.
- Barber hauler marks.
- Marks on the deck running in line with the foot of the jib.
- Calibration strips next to the jib track or track adjusters.

## Jib Height

Try to find a way of attaching the top of the jib consistently so it is the same each time you go sailing. As you rake your mast back you will find the jib gets lower on the deck. Some people compensate for this by moving the jib higher on the wire as they rake back. The decision to do this will depend on your class's ability to move the jib tracks and how much you rake. Personally I think it best to leave the jib height in one position (set correctly for your most upright rake) and let it get lower as you rake back.

## Jib Downhaul (Luff Tension)

In some classes the jib luff is led back so it is easy to adjust, whereas in others it is tied up at the front and so can't easily be adjusted on the water. In most conditions the correct amount of tension (depending on sail and class) is to pull the downhaul tension on until all but the smallest wrinkles are out of the luff of the jib. If you pull more tension on from here it will make the luff of the jib deeper and straighten out the exit of the sail, but if you ease the downhaul it will make a finer entry to the luff and therefore more difficult for the helm to accurately steer to.

## Jib Sheeting

The jib sheet is the most important control; in some classes it is the only control for the jib. Although the jib sheet is in the cleat, the tail should be to hand so it can be adjusted quickly to gusts, lulls or changes in the sea state. When you set the jib up it must be to the right depth at the deck and at the correct leech tension for the jib slot. This is where you have to use both the jib sheets and jib track together to set both correctly.

*It is essential to be consistent with the jib height to keep calibrations accurate .*

## Jib Fairlead Position

In a lot of classes the jib fairlead can be moved forwards and backwards or inboard and outboard by having a block on an adjustable track. Sliding the car forwards on the track will tighten the jib leech because the angle that the jib is sheeted at is getting steeper, so pulling more down the leech and less across the foot. If you slide the car backwards it will do the opposite and the sheeting angle will become shallower, so pulling more across the foot and less down the leech. Jib tracks that slide inwards and outwards work slightly differently. Sliding the jib car inwards will put more return on the bottom battens and tighten the jib slot lower down but will be less effective at closing the upper leech than the fore and aft track. In general the inward and outward tracks are more reliant on the jib sheeting than the fore and aft track to set the upper leech correctly.

It is very important to have everything possible calibrated and clearly marked

# 8 Sail Settings

## The Jib Slot

The jib slot is the most important part of the rig to set up accurately and is also the most sensitive to changes in wind pressure and sea state. Setting the jib slot correctly takes a lot of communication between the helm and crew, as the jib needs to be adjusted at the same time as the mainsail so that they still match up. The jib slot should be at its tightest when you are at maximum power (when you will be fully hiked or trapezing without easing the mainsail), as the wind increases from this point and the boom needs to be eased from the centre, the jib will also need to be eased so that the jib slot is not too tight. Whether you adjust the jib sheet or jib track to do this depends on how deep you want the foot. When the wind decreases from maximum power the jib will have to be eased as well because with less wind passing through the slot it will automatically tighten. The slot should be set further open in choppy water than in flat water because the waves make the boat stop and start and the mainsail will be set fuller, making it more prone to back-winding.

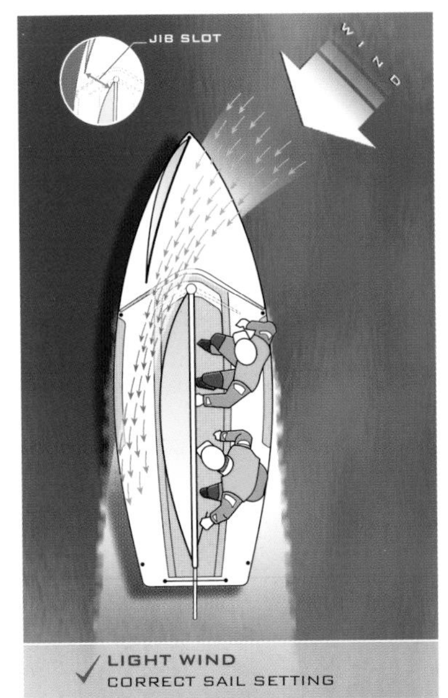


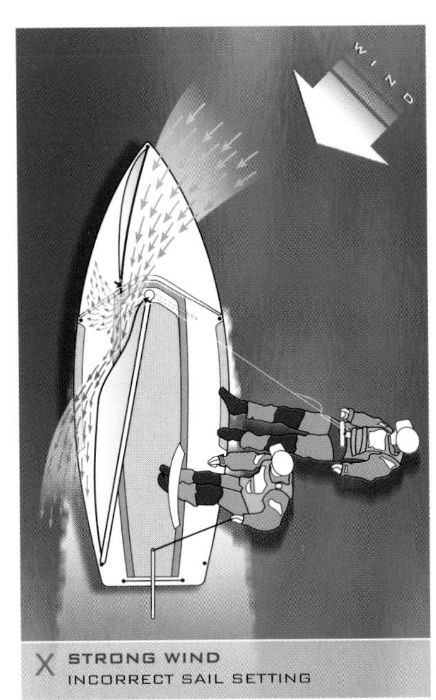


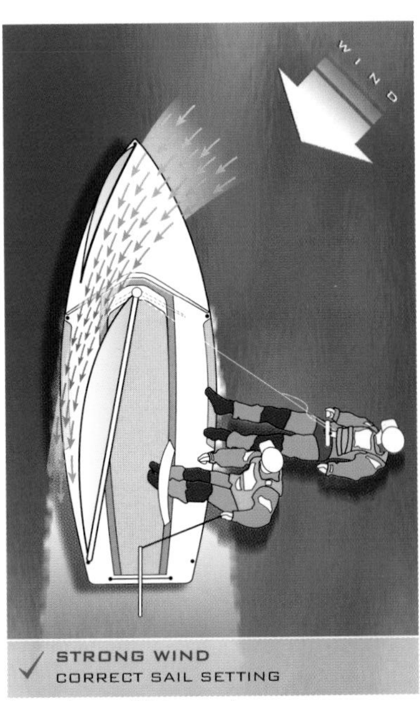


*Illustrations show the effect when the mainsail needs to be eased in a gust, but the jib is not causing the slot to close until it is eased.*

*Jib is eased by moving the fairlead backwards on the track so it matches the eased mainsail for strong winds.*

*Jib slot can be quite tight in these conditions, there is plenty of wind, the water is flat and the boom is on the centre line.*

## Using the Telltales

The telltales are the best tool to make sure you are setting the jib slot correctly. You should have three sets of telltales in from the luff: one in the bottom third, one in the middle and one in the top third. By looking at the windward of these jib telltales you can see if the slot is set correctly. They should be flying horizontally, but when the helm luffs, the top telltale should lift first, followed by the middle and then the bottom telltale. If you can't stop the top telltale from lifting even though the sheet is pulled tight, it means the jib fairlead is too far aft and needs pulling forward.

There should also be telltales a few inches in from the leech in the top quarter of the mainsail and then, parallel with these, some more telltales a few inches in off the luff. If the jib slot is too tight the windward telltale on the mainsail will lift (if the mainsail is set correctly), so the jib sheet will need to be eased or the fairlead let back. The telltale on the jib leech can be used in a similar way, by pulling the jib in until the leeward starts to stall then easing it a tiny amount from here.

*Telltales are the most important tool in setting the jib up correctly, if the jib was too eased the toptell tale would lift vertically whilst if it was too tight the slot would close causing the windward mainsail telltale to droop.*

# 8 Sail Settings

## Setting the Spinnaker

In order to set the spinnaker correctly you will need to trim both the guy and the sheet constantly. This requires a lot of attention from the crew and you won't have time to look around at other things. To trim the spinnaker accurately you need to sit on the windward side of the boat whenever possible. Keeping the boat correctly trimmed will normally require the helm to sit to leeward when sailing on a run. Using the luff of the spinnaker as a guide, ease the sheet and pull around the guy so the luff begins to curl and is on the verge of collapsing, try to keep it in this position so the luff is just curling, without the spinnaker flapping. The amount you adjust the guy depends on the conditions and will usually be less than the amount you adjust the sheet. When you are sailing in planing conditions and the helm is swerving to catch waves the guy will have to be let forward when pointing up, and squared right back when you catch a wave low. If the helm is setting the mainsail correctly the spinnaker pole should normally stay at a similar angle (possibly a couple of degrees further forward) if you line up the boom end with the guy end of the spinnaker pole. If the foot of the spinnaker is pulling tight across the luff of the jib it normally means you are squaring the pole too far round and so you are not able to let enough sheet off without the spinnaker flapping. On a reach you will be less active with the guy, normally cleating it off an inch from the luff of the jib (it is vital to your speed that the pole is not resting on the jib luff!) and simply bowstringing it when you feel you are sailing low enough to square it round. Make sure that, when going from a tight reach to a beam reach, the sheet is eased before you start to square the pole around. This will allow the slot between the spinnaker and mainsail to open, so the main can also be eased.

X INCORRECT
SPINNAKER POLE TOO FAR FORWARD

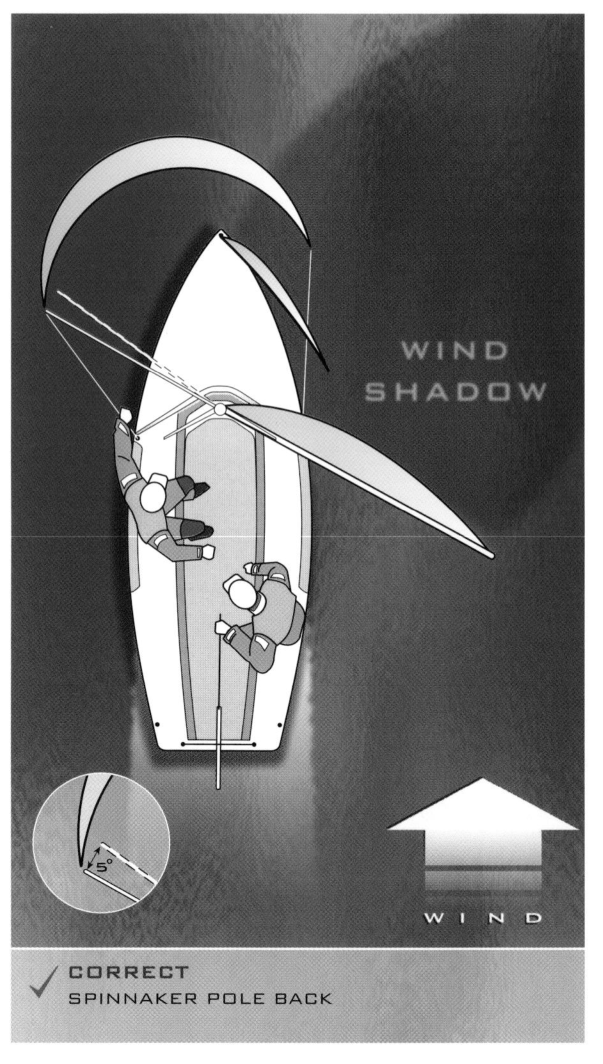


✓ CORRECT
SPINNAKER POLE BACK

## Spinnaker Pole Height

The spinnaker pole height has a big effect on the shape of the spinnaker and how easy it is to trim. The first easy guide to the correct pole height is keeping the spinnaker clews level. In order to achieve this you will need to drop the pole when the wind is light. The luff of the spinnaker is another good indicator of whether you have the correct pole height. If the pole is too high the luff will curl low down first when eased, and when the pole is too low the luff will curl high up first.

*This boat is set up well with good balance, spinnaker squared around and the clews level.*

# 9 Mark Roundings

The same principles apply to fast windward and leeward mark roundings. Try and reduce the amount of tiller used to a minimum and find the right line so you pass the mark on the correct course and as close to it as possible.

## Windward Mark

Make sure you unclip off the trapeze early as you approach the mark and then stay out on your trapeze handle as long as is needed to keep the boat slightly to windward throughout the rounding. It is largely up to the helmsman and their mainsheet control to keep the boat at the right angle, and as a crew there is a fair amount of trust involved that they won't dunk you! It is really important when bearing away onto a run to try and gain a boat length to windward of the mark on the approach as this will allow you to bear away smoothly and still be on the right angle and as close to the mark as possible on exit.

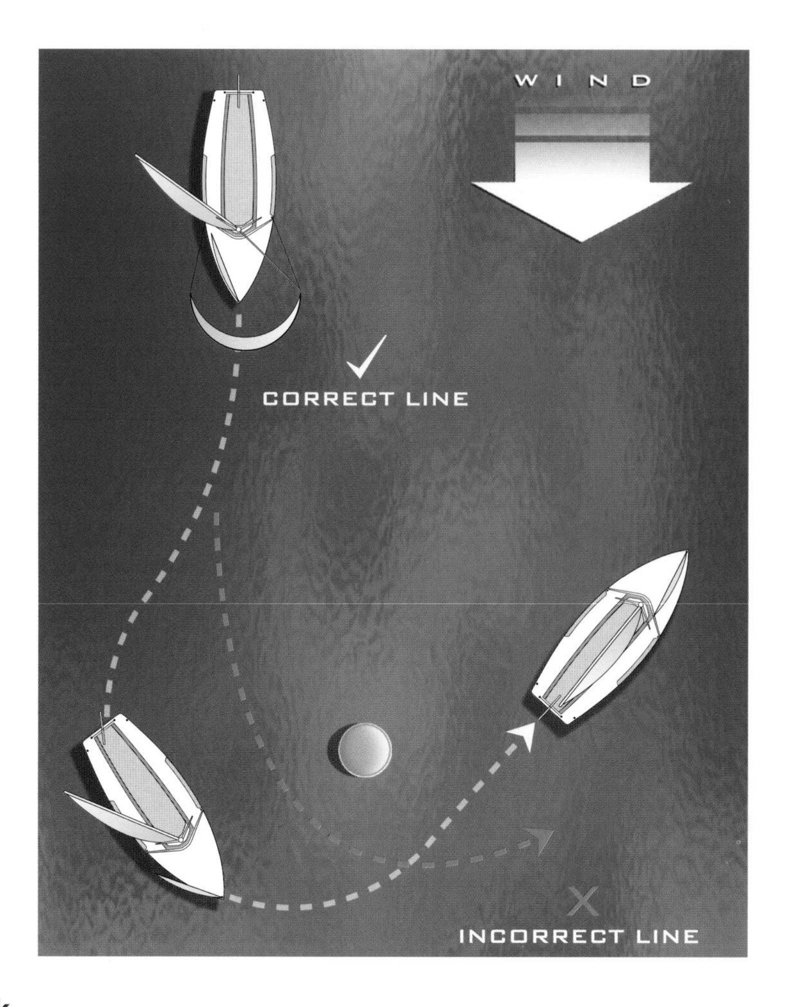


## Leeward Mark

One of the most common mistakes crews make at leeward marks is bringing the jib in too early; remember doing this will make the boat want to bear away just as you are trying to point up. The jib should be pulled in, synchronized with the mainsail. The boat will need to be allowed to heel to leeward as you point up, the amount will depend on the class and wind strength (more leeward heel in less wind), if possible leave enough room between you and the mark so you have completed your turn onto close hauled by the time you round the mark. If it is trapezing conditions you have the problem of the mark hitting your body as you round, normally in marginal trapezing conditions it is best to delay going out on the trapeze until after the rounding and take the windward gain by being closer to the mark. Once in flat trapezing conditions you should allow enough room for your crouched body to trapeze as the extra leverage will gain you more speed and you can use this to give you the height after the rounding.

*When rounding the windward mark control the small amount of windward heel by holding yourself on the handle.*

# 10 Using the Spinnaker

## The Spinnaker Pole

Your spinnaker pole should have a means of attaching both ends to the mast or guy, and the middle to an adjustable uphaul–downhaul system. The jaws at each end of the pole can point up or down; it is a personal choice. I prefer the jaws to be pointing up as I find it quicker to drop the pole than raise it. There should be a bit of thin string between the ends of the pole that has a tiny amount of slack in it when both ends are closed. Check the length of your pole compared to the class rules; usually it should be full length.

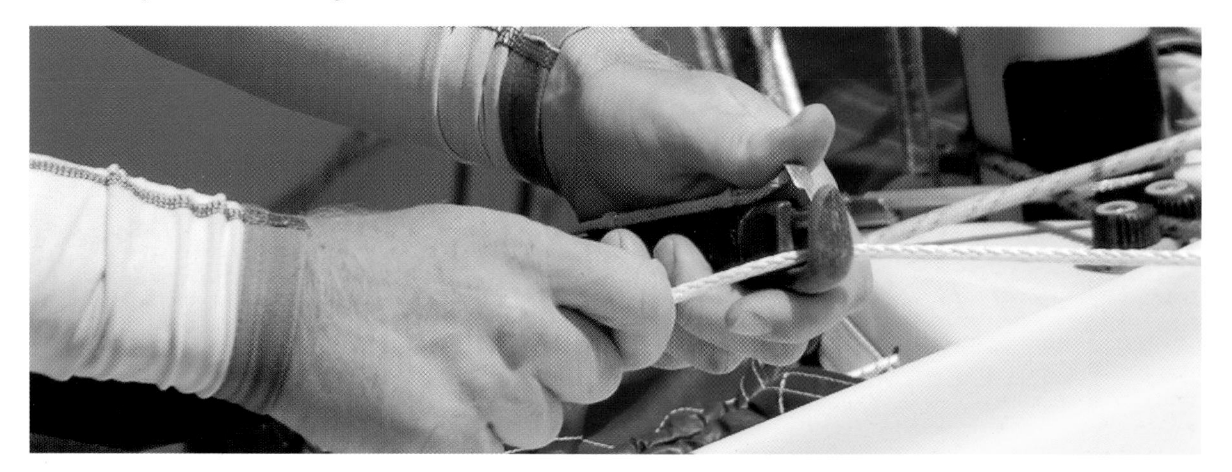

## Using a Spinnaker Pole

The success of your spinnaker manoeuvre relies heavily on the speed at which you can do your 'pole work' and settle down to sailing the boat fast again. There are many different spinnaker-pole systems on different classes, but the principles remain the same.

When using the pole, hold it at the end you are trying to clip on, so that you have complete control (especially if the spinnaker is flapping and the pole is bouncing around). While bringing the pole out or in you should keep it between yourself and the mast so that you can still move your weight to windward in a gust if required. When pushing the pole out, clip it onto the guy first then onto the hook or ramp (depending on the system) and then finally onto the loop mast.

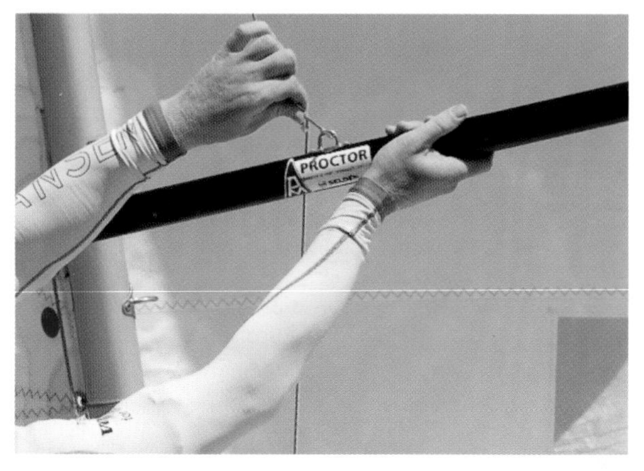


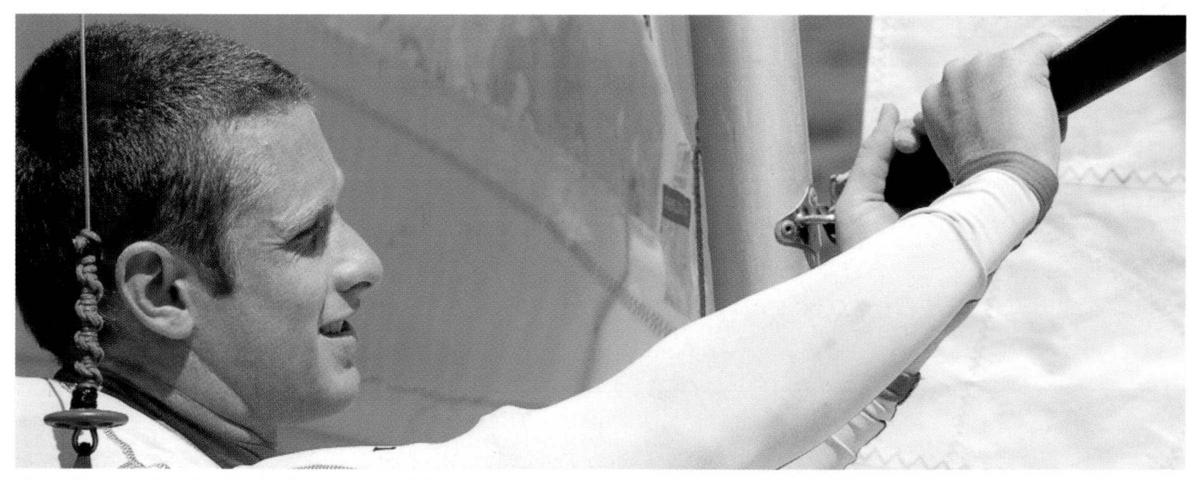

*Use both hands close together to clip onto the guy' 2 'Push the pole out and bring the hook out to the pole'. 'When you clip the pole onto the mast it can bounce around if the spinnaker is up so use both hands and a swift firm movement.*

## Running the Tapes

As a crew it is your responsibility to make sure the spinnaker will go up cleanly without twists. Before the start of a race, run your hand from the head to the clew down the leech of the spinnaker whose sheet runs around the front of the jib. Check there are no twists and carefully pack it in the bag with the head on the top and clip the halyard away.

The string on the pole is used when unclipping the pole during either a gybe or a drop. By bowstringing the string close to the mast-end of the pole you should be able to make both ends unclip without even touching the pole itself. During a drop you would then take it off the middle before bringing the pole into the boat.

*In light winds the pole will need to be lowered to keep the clews level. If there is no pressure in the spinnaker then get the helm to head up slightly.*

# 10 Using the Spinnaker

## See Training Exercises 1 & 6

## Hoisting onto a Run

Try to get as many things done before the windward mark-rounding as possible. This will be easier in light winds because you won't be trapezing or leaning out. The main thing is to get the guy pulled around and cleated in the right position for a reach (the spinnaker will fall out of the bag if you pull it around far enough for a run). You should have marks on the sheets so that this is possible. If you have twinning lines make sure the windward one is on, if not, put the guy under the reaching hook. Sometimes it is even possible to get the pole half or completely on in light conditions.

Once the rounding is completed, the helm should be making sure everything is set up for the run and the boat is sailing the best Velocity Made Good (VMG), while, as a crew, you need to start putting the pole on. Once you have clipped the pole onto the guy and the middle onto the hook, call to your helm to start the hoist. As soon as the helm starts to hoist, push the pole out onto the mast and immediately reach for the sheet. Provided the guy is already preset, the spinnaker should fill.

ROGERS
GLANFIELD

1

GBR
GBR
ROGERS
GLANFIELD

2

GBR
GBR
ROGERS
GLANFIELD

3

GBR
GBR
ROGERS
GLANFIELD

4

ROGERS
GLANFIELD

5

# 10 Using the Spinnaker

## See Training Exercise 6

## Gybe-Set Hoist

Often it is not possible to prepare for a gybe set, but if you get the chance, pre-set the twinners and guy before rounding the windward mark. Failing that, do it after rounding before you go for the pole.

Accurate steering is essential for a good gybe set. Even if you have to hold height after the gybe to defend your wind it is vital to bear away onto a square run for the moment you hoist the spinnaker. I have never been keen on doing 'chucker' hoists (where the crew throws the spinnaker around the front of the jib as the helm hoists) – I think they are slow, inconsistent and risky. If the helm delays the hoist a couple of seconds so the crew can clip the pole onto the guy, it should be possible to hoist the spinnaker straight from the windward bag. As the spinnaker goes up, the crew can push the pole out and help the spinnaker around the forestay. The pole will give the spinnaker some stability and help the helm set it. For this reason it is important to then bring the hook out to the middle of the pole rather than the pole in to the hook.

*A tight rounding is important whilst racing to avoid getting rolled.*

1

2

*Here I use the pole to help push the spinnaker around the front of the forestay.*

3

# 10 Using the Spinnaker

## See Training Exercise 5

## Hoisting onto a Reach

A common mistake while hoisting onto a reach is to rush into hoisting the spinnaker before all the preparation work is done. Remember, having a flapping spinnaker hoisted is slower than no spinnaker at all, so don't go for the hoist until you are confident it will set soon after. As with the other types of hoist, try to get as many things as possible done before the windward mark. If there are trapezing conditions you should still be able to pull the twinner on or get the guy under the reaching clip.

As a crew you should also locate the wing mark before the rounding. While you round, check you are not in danger of getting rolled (if you are, stay out and sail high to defend your wind), then come in and go for the pole. Meanwhile, the helm should keep the boat balanced and make sure it is set up for a reach. Once the pole is clipped onto the guy and the uphaul–downhaul system, call back to the helm that you are ready. At this point he can bear away and hoist. In the time the helm takes to hoist the spinnaker you should be able to clip the pole onto the mast and reach back to the sheet to set the spinnaker.

1

2

3

4

5

6

*With practice you should be able to go onto the trapeze using the handle with the spinnaker sheet in the other hand, you can then clip on once you are out there.* **7**

# 10 Using the Spinnaker

## See Training Exercise 6

## Using a Spinnaker Chute

There is not a big difference in your boat-handling when using a spinnaker chute. The main difference when hoisting is that there is no windward or leeward hoist. When dropping, you can usually leave it later than you would with a spinnaker bag, as in most cases the helm can drop the kite while the crew does the pole. Tension should be kept on the sheet to prevent it falling under the bow.

## See Training Exercises 4 & 6

## Gybing

There are many different ways to gybe, and the technique will vary according to the type of boat and the wind strength. It is important to have a good standard gybe that you can vary slightly for very light winds and very strong winds.

For the standard gybe that you would expect to use most of the time, I prefer to keep the preparation to a minimum so that the gybe is not signalled to competitors. For this reason I always leave doing the jib and pole until after the gybe.

Just before the helm starts to steer into the gybe, you will need to transfer the spinnaker sheets to him or her. This needs to be done quickly but very carefully so that the spinnaker does not flap. The best way is for the crew to let off the twinner or take it out of the reaching hook while the helm takes up the slack on the guy so the pole does not move forward. The helm also takes the sheet in the other hand immediately after taking the slack out of the guy. It is a helm's choice whether they put the tiller between their knees to steer or hold it in their hand (the hand that is on the new leeward side after the gybe). If they put it between their knees it leaves their hands free, but holding the extension in their hand allows them to move forward in the boat and gives them greater freedom of movement.

Once the helm has control of the spinnaker sheets, pull down the leeward twinner (not needed if you have reaching hooks) so it is preset for the opposite tack then, in conjunction with the helm's steering, pull the boom across by the kicker. Usually, once it is across you should give it a small pump to make sure all the battens have flicked through to the new side. As you move through the boat, uncleat the jib so it is not backed. When you go for the spinnaker pole, grab it by the string at the mast end with your hand that is closest; if you bowstring it the pole should uncleat off the mast and the old guy simultaneously. You can then swing it across and clip it onto the new guy and mast.

1

2

3

4

5

6

7

## Light Wind Gybing

Often in light winds you will be sailing higher angles downwind than in medium winds, and this will affect the gybing technique. The helm might need to preset the mainsail in the cleat if it is not resting on the shroud, and an extra effort will need to be made to swing the spinnaker from one side to the other through the gybe so it is set correctly for the new tack. More roll will be needed to help the boat steer through the gybe. This can be induced by the crew staying on the windward side for longer or the helm moving across from the leeward side and leaning his or her weight on the windward side.

As with all light-wind sailing, moving smoothly across the boat is essential. When doing the pole, try to find a balance between being fast and not clattering around. Even if you do a roll-gybe, try to leave bringing the boat flat until after the crew has completed the pole. This will keep the boat sailing smoothly and the leeward heel will help the sails fill under their own weight.

## See Training Exercises 2 & 6

## Heavy Wind Gybing

The priority during a heavy-wind gybe is to go into it at maximum speed, when there is the least amount of pressure on the rig. This means you don't need much preparation, so you can keep maximum speed on and do it down a wave. The biggest difference between a standard gybe and heavy-wind gybe (or safety gybe, as we call it) is that the helm pulls the boom over by holding the mainsheets together (not possible in boats with no purchases or aft mainsheet). This makes it easier to pull the boom across than if the crew holds it at the kicker, and easier to time correctly with the helm's steering. The helm does not get up off the leeward tank when doing this and is therefore already sitting on the windward side once the boom has come across, which allows the helm to sail higher and use his or her weight to keep the boat upright. Before the gybe, the helm will do the same as in the standard gybe, taking the slack out of the guy, ready to keep it set when you let go. The difference is, you don't let the twinner go until you start to move in, then, as you don't have to pull the boom across, you can let the old twinner off, let go of the spinnaker sheet and pull the new twinner on while moving through the boat. The jib will also need to be uncleated. When you go for the pole on the new side it is essential you are as fast as possible, ideally finishing before the boat has fallen off the wave you gybed on. The longer you are standing at the front of the boat, the more likely the nose of the boat is to dig in

*Go into the gybe at maximum speed and get the helm to pull the boom across.*

*Be as quick as possible doing the pole on the new side, when you will be the most vulnerable to capsize.*

*The helm is sat a long way aft to counteract my weight at the mast, his weight is also outboard so he can sail a higher angle reducing the risk of the bow digging in.*

## Dropping the Spinnaker

The age-old mistake with spinnaker drops is not leaving enough time before the leeward mark. This is a particularly costly mistake in trapeze boats as it delays the crew moving out onto the trapeze after the rounding. Most delays are due to a tangle in the halyard, so make sure you or the helm checks it in plenty of time before the drop. The next area for occasional problems is dropping the pole. There is actually no reason why this can't be done fairly early as, if the helm is in control of the spinnaker, he or she should be able to keep it set for a few seconds without the pole on. When you go for the pole, make sure the helm has the sheets first then, at the mast end, grab the string at the top of the pole and bowstring it to release the end attached to the mast and the end attached to the guy simultaneously. Swing the pole in between you and the mast, unclipping it from the middle as you go, and stow it in the boat. When you reach for the spinnaker, pull the foot around first so that the sheet will not fall under the bow, then, in large reaches, drop the rest and tuck in what remains of the foot.

If you are approaching the leeward mark on the wrong tack and you have to gybe at the mark, give yourself much more time to drop the spinnaker, not only because you then have to fit a gybe in, but also because if there are any delays, missing the mark will have even worse consequences. There is rarely need to do a pole-off gybe-and-drop I would always try to avoid this, instead doing it all before or after the gybe.

*Use large armpulls to get the spinnaker down quickly and when you have finished make sure it is clipped away with the sheets tidy to avoid problems whilst sailing up wind.*

# 10 Using the Spinnaker

# Using the Spinnaker 10

# 11 Downwind Technique

## See Training Exercises 4 & 6

The downwind legs of a race offer massive opportunities to gain both distance and places. As the standard of racing improves, the opportunities to gain upwind are significantly reduced compared to the opportunities downwind. This is because the technique downwind is complicated and very specific to changes in wind speed or sea state and, unlike the upwind legs, if you are behind you are able to cover and attack.

## Light Wind Running

Running in wind so light that you have to sail angles in order to set the spinnaker is very different from running when there is enough wind to sail low with the spinnaker setting. When this happens depends on the size of the spinnaker and speed of the boat. If the wind is so light you are having to sail angles, make sure the boat is set up for a broad reach rather than a run. The helm brings the mainsail in until it stops back-winding, and pulls some centreboard down, and the crew lets the guy forward. The boat needs to be sailed with a small amount of leeward heel, so the sails will set on their own weight, and to help the spinnaker fly away from the boat. Both the helm and crew should be well forward in the boat and then be as gentle and still as possible.

In these light conditions the communication between the helm and crew is essential to finding the best VMG. The crew should be telling the helm about the 'weight' in the spinnaker, advising if the helm could sail a lower angle and still keep the spinnaker pulling. It is then up to the helm to decide whether it is best to sail lower. The crew can also tell the helm if they feel the boat has been lifted or headed from a wind shift.

Once the boat is sailing on a dead run the spinnaker can be squared round and the boat brought flat or slightly to windward. This will give the tiller neutral helm so a minimal amount of rudder needs to be used. It will also reduce the wetted surface of the hull.

## Medium Wind Running

The one thing that will most affect your medium-wind technique is whether you are sailing a set VMG angle or are swerving to catch and plane down waves. This will depend on the sea state. If you are still sailing a straight VMG angle, not much will change from your light-wind technique. You might be able to square the spinnaker around further, this then means that where the helm sets the kicker will become important: not enough will lose power and make the boat more unstable, but too much will prevent it from sailing low.

If you are swerving to catch waves the boat balance becomes essential. Bringing the boat to windward when bearing away and to leeward when pointing up reduces the amount of tiller used and allows you to turn sharply. You can use both the sail settings and your body weight to control the balance of the boat. I always try to find something to put my feet under (usually the centreboard case) so that I can lean out when needed and pull myself in quickly when I need to get my weight inboard. You will also need to have the ability to move forwards and backwards in the boat despite the fact that holding the guy will restrict how far back you can move. You should be keeping an eye on the waves next to you as well as on the spinnaker, trying to anticipate when the helm will head up and bear away.

Now that you are able to plane you can use one pump per wave to promote planing. When pumping the spinnaker, make sure you pump both the guy and sheet together. The pumping can be aggressive and quick but it is the timing that is the most important thing. There is a lot to co-ordinate in planing conditions and it easy to make it more complicated than it is. The best thing is to break it down into steps.

- Point the boat up to gain speed with your weight out and forward and the sails in.
- As you feel the wave pick the transom up, pump the sails and let the boat come over to windward, bearing away down the wave.
- Once planing, slide your weight back with the mainsail fully eased and spinnaker squared around.
- Before you hit the wave in front, use the speed you are at to point up again, allowing the boat to heel slightly to leeward and just before you do so pull in the sails and slide forward, ready for the next wave.

If you are going slowly, invariably you have made the technique too complicated and you need to break it down and get your timing right.

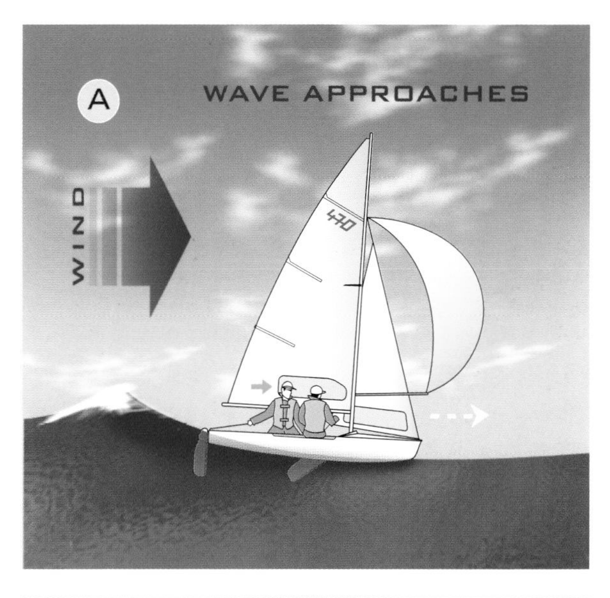

*When sailing downwind in big waves you are literally trying to surf the waves. As the wave approaches you need to be well forward trying to build speed. Once the wave is under you slide backwards and sail across the waves face so you don't hit the wave in front.*

*In strong winds make sure you can change your position easily. Here I have my feet under the centre board case, I can use it to hike off or quickly pull myself in.*

## Heavy Wind Running

There are two main styles when sailing in strong winds, and which one you use depends on whether or not you are travelling faster than the waves. If the waves are faster than you the technique is similar to that for medium winds: to try to catch a wave and stay on it as long as possible. If you are faster than the waves you will need to find a way over them. This usually means more weight up to windward and holding a much steadier course. With both techniques you will have to move your weight much further back than in medium winds. This might make it difficult for you to play the guy, in which case you should play it through the cleat behind the reaching hook. The boat needs to be flat to prevent a roll to windward or a broach. I often clip myself onto the trapeze so I am ready if we need to head up for a wave or to avoid another boat.

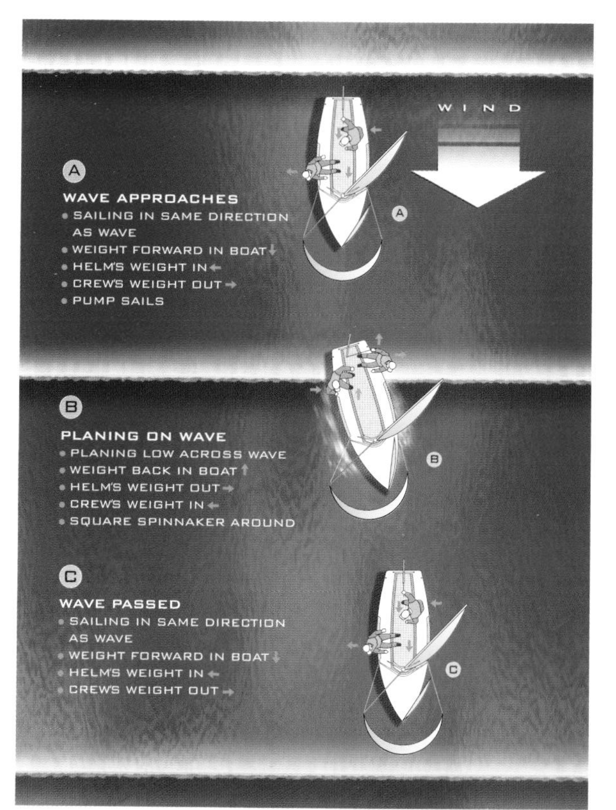


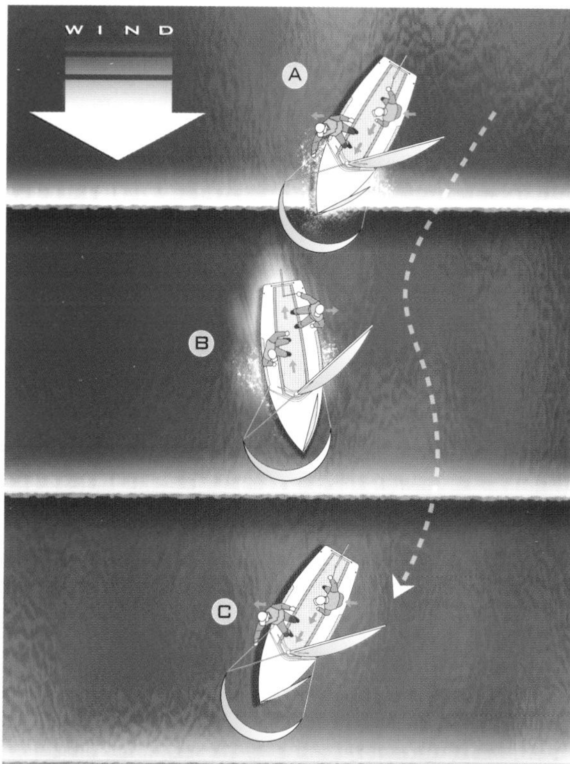

*If the bow is digging into the wave hold the guy behind the reaching hook so you can then move backwards but still pump.*

## Reaching

**Exercise 5**

There is less technique involved on a reach than a run, but a reach is a very important leg of the course when setting yourself up for a run. If you gain a couple of boat-lengths on the boat in front you can be in a position to attack them on the run.

The windward and leeward trim is important down a run to keep the right balance on the rudder. Most boats are prone to some lee helm when reaching because of the spinnaker flying at the front of the boat and the fact the centreboard is half-lifted. This makes it very important not to let the boat come to windward, and the correct trim is normally flat or with a tiny amount of leeward heel.

Before planing conditions you are looking to balance the boat fore and aft so there is maximum waterline length. Once you are planing, the fore and aft trim will make a big difference to whether the boat wants to sail high or low. If you are trying to plane low, taking a step back will lift the bow and blow it off the wind, pushing you lower. If you are trying to point higher you will need to step forward to get more boat in the water and reduce the lee helm.

*'When trapezing on a reach your fore and aft trim will make a huge difference to your speed and the feel of the boat.*

*Left: This boat looks well set up, but on closer inspection the centreboard is too far down, this will cause stagger and make it harder to get on the plane.*

# 12 Rule 42 Class Exceptions

## See Training Exercises 2 and 4

More and more classes have made propulsion (other than the one pump to induce planing) legal above a certain wind condition. This is normally signalled by hoisting a flag at start time or in some cases at a mark during the race. This completely changes the downwind technique, making it much more physical and giving the sailor more options in how to use the sails and body weight to propel the boat.

There are four main things you can do that you could not do before:

1. Repetitive pumping (one pump after the other in quick succession).
2. Rocking (pulling the boat flat quickly, by fanning the sails).
3. Ooching (moving your body weight forwards in sharp, jerky movements).
4. Bouncing on the trapeze wire (pulling your hips down to flick the leech of the main and pull the boat flat in gusts).

All four of these methods can be used together but, as before, the most important thing is the rhythm and timing. It is very easy to put a lot of effort in and pump yourself slower!

With plenty of weight up to windward you can pump repeatedly on the mainsail and spinnaker to gain hull speed quicker

*Even when pumping aggressively and in quick succession try not to lose sight of the rhythm and balance.*

## Repetitive Pumping

Being able to pump repeatedly causes the biggest change when pointing up, either to get speed to catch a wave, or to sail over a wave. With plenty of weight up to windward you can pump repeatedly on the mainsail and spinnaker to gain hull speed quicker, making it easier to catch a wave and sail lower once you are on it. The same principle applies to when you can pump only once: both the guy and sheet should be pumped together and timed with the helm's mainsail pump.

## Ooching

Ooching is a useful way to stay low on a wave when you are already planing and have little power in the spinnaker or mainsail to pump with. Making sharp movements forward, pressing against a fixed object in the boat can be just enough to keep the boat on the wave when it was about to fall behind.

**See Training Exercise 5**

## On a Reach

Most of the pumping on a strong-wind reach will have to come from the helmsman if the crew is trapezing. The crew making small pumps on the sheet can help but pumping on both the guy and the sheet can be difficult and make the boat feel unstable if already planing. There is the opportunity to ooch by moving forward suddenly if you are close to getting down a wave.

## Rocking

It is useful to use rocking when sailing in the medium-wind VMG condition, holding a steady course but consistently rocking the boat in time with a gentle pump. Rocking is also a good way to improve the bear-away when you are about to surf down the wave.

**See Training Exercise 3**

## Bouncing on the Trapeze Wire

This technique can be used on a reach or while sailing upwind. Its effectiveness depends on the type of centreboard your class has. If the board is narrow, bouncing on the trapeze will knock the boat sideways and do more harm than good. To do it you simply pull your hips down in a quick action, it can be a good technique in sudden gusts or when at the top of a wave sailing upwind or on a reach.

# 13 High Performance Dinghy Sailing

'High-performance' is a label that has been given to describe a relatively new range of fast, powerful classes characterized by asymmetric spinnakers and skiff-shape hulls. Crewing in high-performance dinghies requires slightly different skills from those used in a 'conventional' dinghy. Because racing is held over short windward-to-leeward courses and the boats tend to be unstable and early to plane there is high emphasis on good boat-handling, which is harder to achieve in this class than in most racing dinghies.

The following are some of the broader skills you need at advanced level in order to be a successful high-performance crew.

*Good upper body strength, aerobic fitness and agility are essential for a top high performance crew.*

## Communication

The black art of good communication is often the skill that separates the good from the average. Complicated and precise boat-handling demands that all manoeuvres need to be planned and well timed. You will find that sailing on short courses with fast boats entails many variables coming at you very quickly so, to make sure they are all being dealt with, you will need clear roles and constant talking to keep each other briefed. In twin-trapeze boats it is easier to discuss tactics than in single-trapeze boats, as your heads are closer together and you share the same vantage point and outlook from the boat.

## Boat Balance

Your primary job as a high-performance crew is undoubtedly to make sure the boat is well balanced at all times, and you will need a detailed understanding of what your movements will do to the 'helm' (feel) on the rudder. There is a very small margin for error on the windward/leeward heel before the rudder becomes ineffective at steering the boat, so without the correct boat trim you will not only be slow but the helmsman will struggle to steer around the course at all! The fore and aft trim is equally important, as it also affects the 'helm' on the rudder. Through all the boat-handling manoeuvres the balance remains your prime responsibility, and in stronger winds you need to always be ready to drop what you are doing and help the helm keep the boat flat.

## Sail Settings and Rig Adjustments

In most single-trapeze boats the layout will make things convenient for the helm to make the adjustments so that the crew does not need to move off the trapeze. In a twin-trapeze boat, ideally, the controls should be laid out to be convenient for the crew. Both the helm and the crew are on the trapeze, so it makes sense to leave the helm to concentrate on the steering and the crew to make adjustments. In a number of classes the crew is allowed to take the main straight from the boom. This is thought to be faster, not so much because of the loads on the sheet, but more because the crew can use both hands to play it and react quickly to gusts and lulls. It puts the crew in the unusual position of being responsible for the main setting and, without a cleat, needs constant attention.

## Physical Fitness

Crewing in a high-performance boat requires a high level of fitness, the boat-handling manoeuvres are particularly physically demanding. To be successful you will need a high level of aerobic fitness, good upper body strength, agility and flexibility.

## See Training Exercises 1 & 6

## Boat Handling

The boat handling manoeuvres explained here are specifically for twin trapeze, asymmetric boats with a skiff design hull because it is completely different to the other boat handling section in this book. If the class of boat you sail is somewhere in between you can pick out the bits that are relative.

*The crew often takes the mainsheet upwind and has to keep a high level of concentration on the balance.*

*Downwind the helm takes the mainsheet while the crew controls the kite.*

See Training Exercise 8

## Tacking

When tacking a skiff boat you usually have a long way to travel to get across the boat so when you come in off the trapeze you need to lift yourself into a standing position so you can run across the boat, your movements should be synchronized with the helm moving across the boat. If you are holding the mainsheet be careful not to let too much mainsail out as you move in which will reduce the weather helm just as you want to point up. The mainsheet should be held in your aft hand whilst you unhook with your bow hand, As you move across the centre of the boat transfer the mainsheet to your other hand behind your back whilst facing forward so you go out on the trapeze handle with your bow hand. Once both the helm and crew are trapezing you should tack the boat relatively flat and it is literally a flat out run across the boat and straight into maximum leverage on the new side. In lighter winds you can allow the boat to roll slightly before moving across the boat, when you bring the boat flat on the new side it is essential you get your weight forward immediately and in very light winds be prepared to tack in front of the mast.

1

2

3

4

5

*The helm and crew should move across the boat at the same time with the crew changing hands holding the mainsheet behind their back.* 6

# 13 High Performance Dinghy Sailing

## The Bear Away and Hoist

As you are approaching the windward mark there is a certain amount of preparation that needs to be done. The spinnaker sheet needs the slack pulled through as it won't be held by anyone whilst the asymmetric is being hoisted. In light winds the crew will pass the mainsheet to the helm and take the jib sheet which you ease steadily as you start to bear away. In stronger winds, when there is a benefit to having two hands on the mainsheet the crew will take it, easing it through the bear away so the boat is slightly to windward all the way then passing it to the helm as you come in for the hoist. When you go for the bearaway you will need to move your weight back to keep the bow from digging into a wave and be prepared for a quick change of course, in strong winds there will be quite strong G-forces pulling you forwards. As you move in go straight for the hoist taking up a wide balanced stance with legs slightly bent and back lowered go for quick arm over arm pulls to get the kite up. Remember there is a huge difference in speed between a boat with or without the kite up so the speed of the hoist is essential. Once you have completed the hoist grab the sheet and go straight out on the trapeze clipping on when you are out there (this will take practice, sometimes if there is a lot of power in the sheet, you need the helm to clip you on whilst you hold onto the handle).

1

2

3

4

5

*Speed is of the essence when it comes to hoisting the spinnaker, the speed differences with or without the spinnaker are huge so the quicker it can go up the quicker you can get planing.*

6

## Gybing

Gybing an asymmetric class boat is actually a lot easier and more efficient than gybing with a conventional spinnaker; there is less to do before and after the gybe so it is easier to go quickly from maximum leverage on one side to maximum leverage on the new side which in turn keeps boat speed up.

To avoid the rig loading up you should always be at maximum speed when you go for a gybe. As you come in off the trapeze try to avoid easing the asymmetric sheet too much, if anything pull it in slightly, then once you are in the middle of the boat pick up the new sheet and rapidly sheet it in hand after hand. It is essential at all times that you keep control of the asymmetric clew, never letting too much slack in one of the sheets so it can fly away from the boat. As you move up on the windward side, the helm will be heading up, the asymmetric should be slightly over-sheeted and once you are out on the trapeze handle bring the loop to the trapeze hook whilst allowing the sheet to slowly run through your hand so the spinnaker sets as you hook on.

1

2

3

4

*Always stay in control of the aysmmetric clew never letting out too much sheet allowing it to fly along way from the boat.*

HH
HELLY HANSEN

## Dropping

On an asymmetric boat you can leave the drop till much closer to the mark compared to a conventional spinnaker, there is no pole to take down and the difference in boat speed between having the asymmetric set and not is greater than a boat with a conventional spinnaker.

As you come in off the trapeze try and stand on the asymmetric sheet keeping the kite filling as you start to take up the slack on the downhaul, once the slack is taken up uncleat the halyard and rapidly pull arm over arm on the downhaul. As you move up onto the windward side take the jib sheet, pulling it in as you move, once you have rounded and are hooked onto the trapeze take the mainsheet off the helm and hand him the jib sheet, which should be joined at the end.

1

2

3

4

5

# 14 Starting

The start is undoubtedly the most important part of the race, and is also the most complicated in terms of communication and co-ordination between helm and crew.

## See Training Exercise 7


## Preparation

The first thing you need to do is find out which end of the line is bias. The most accurate and useful way to do this is by using your compass. Start at the starboard end of the line and sail towards the port end so you are sailing exactly down the line, take a bearing at the port end, then go head-to-wind and take another bearing. You then subtract the port bearing from the head-to-wind bearing. If the answer is 90 degrees the line is square (no end is bias), if less than 90° the port end is bias and if more than 90° the starboard end is bias. The advantage of using a compass is that it puts an actual figure on the bias: if it is 5 degrees you might decide it is not worth fighting at the favoured end, whereas if it is 20 degrees you probably won't be able to afford to miss it. The other advantage of using a compass is that when you go head-to-wind you can check the heading against the mean reading you got early in the pre-start when you were doing your upwind compass numbers. There is no point in figuring out you have 5 degrees port bias without realizing you are in a 20-degree-left phase!

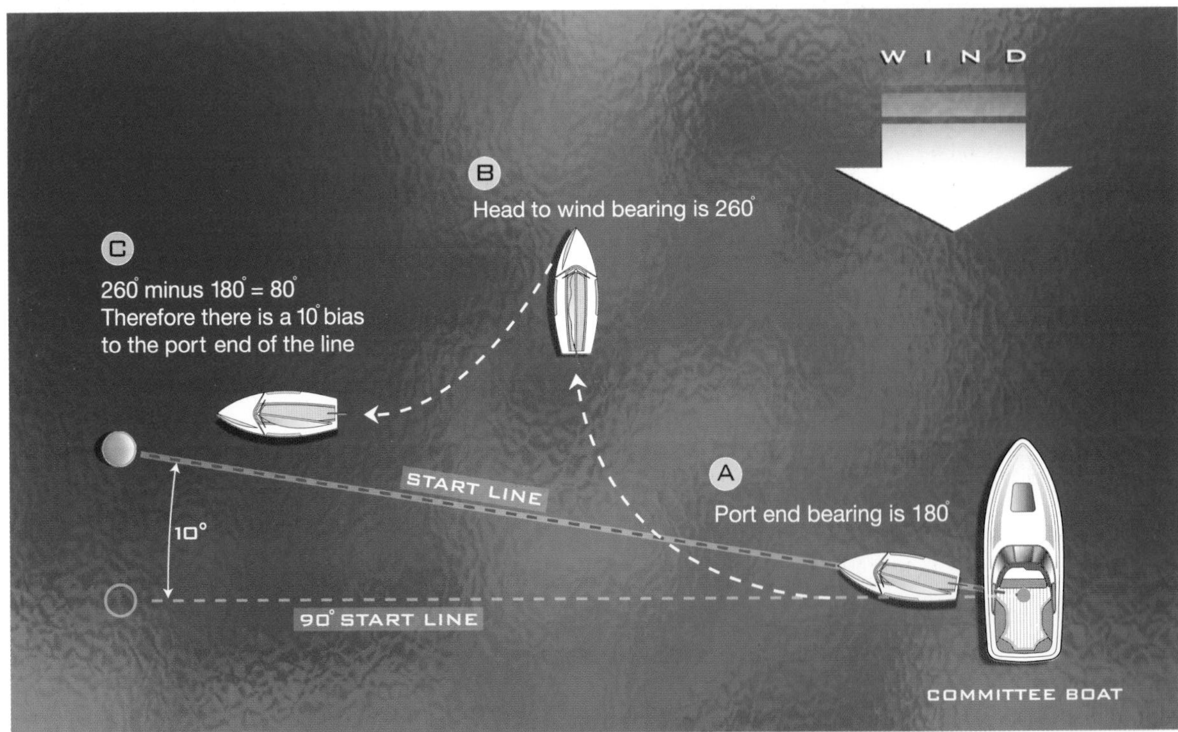


*This illustration shows the process of finding the line bias using a compass. First taking the line bearing, then the head to wind bearing and finally working out the difference between the two.*

The next thing to do is to get a transit so you can tell when you are close to the start line. Normally this is easiest to do towards the port end of the line, although it can be useful to get one off the starboard end as well. Do this by sailing next to the starboard end, so you are on the line, and align the port end with something distinctive on the shore. An exact transit is of limited use, though, as it is hard to see while you are queuing a few boat-lengths back from the line, and when you are on it your bow will be over it, so you need a safe transit as well. A safe transit is when you line up something on the shore with the port end that will put you a certain distance behind the line. To get this, sail two boat-lengths behind the line at the starboard end and see what this lines up with on the shore. Remember, if you got your safe transit from two boat-lengths behind the line at the starboard end, when you are on the same transit halfway down the line you will be only one boat-length behind the line, and at the pin end the distance you are behind will be negligible. If you are going to be queuing early and a long way back it can be worth getting a third, even safer, transit or, failing that, just get very familiar with the land in front of your safe transit.

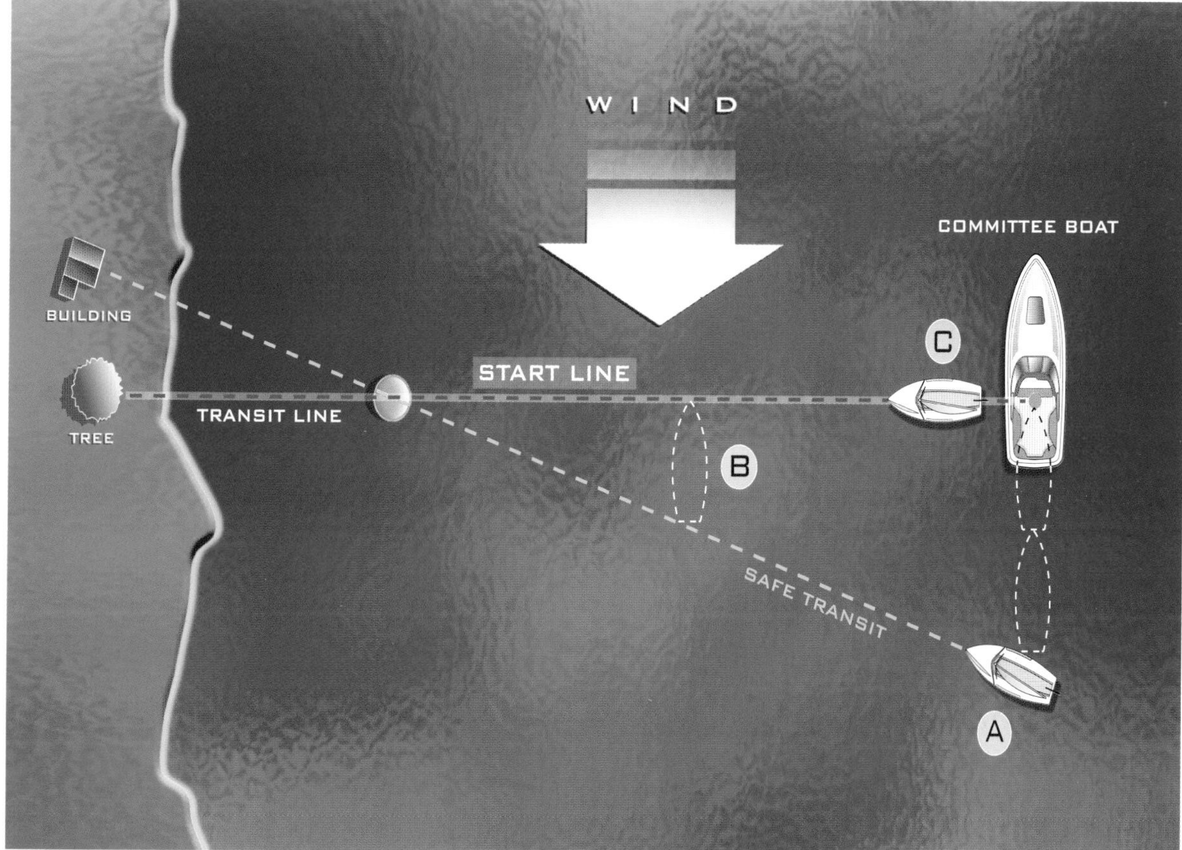


*You should get an exact and a safe transit, you will find the safe transit is easier to see pre-start and will help to judge acceleration. Remember if your safe transit puts you two boat lengths back at the opposite end you will only be one boat length back in the middle.*

## Starting Roles

There are a number of tasks that need to be taken care of in the final minutes of pre-start. Who does what will vary from boat to boat and, while there is no set way things should be done, it is important that both helm and crew know clearly what they are meant to be doing. It makes sense that the helm does the jobs where a quick response on the tiller is needed, and that the crew is doing the jobs that require a high level of concentration (as they don't have to concentrate on steering).

## See Training Exercises 1 & 3

## Starting Jobs

- Counting down time untill start.
- Watching port-end transit and calling the distance from the line.
- Watching starboard-end transit (if you have one) and calling the distance from the line.
- Looking for approaching boats on port.
- Looking for approaching boats on starboard.
- Watching for changes in wind speed and direction coming down the course (important in unstable winds).
- Calling the final acceleration to the line.

# 14 Starting

## Risk Management

One of the biggest decisions you have to make when starting is the priority you put on it and how far you are willing to push and risk OCS in order to gain a good start. Your decision will be based on a complicated calculation of a number of variables, but it should be consciously made and the risk you are willing to take agreed between the team. For instance, on a shifty, gusty day when there will be lots of chances for position changes and big gains, it would be stupid to push the start as much as when there is a steady wind and little to be gained or lost. Other things to consider are whether the prevailing conditions suit your strengths or expose your weaknesses: if they expose a weakness your chances of recovery from a bad start are quite poor. Towards the end of the regatta it is worth considering what result you need in order to attain your goal. The final thing that will affect your risk management is how confident you are of your position on the line. If it is a day when there are no decent visible transits you would be wise to use a bit of caution and not stick out in front of the fleet.

## See Training Exercise 1

## Acceleration

Accelerating for the line is a complicated process. Here are a few tips to consider:

- Position yourself so you have a good gap to leeward and are close to the boat to windward.
- Make sure you are not head-to-wind or have not completely stopped when you start the acceleration as this makes it harder to judge the amount of time it will take you to reach full speed.
- Pull the jib in momentarily before the main. This will help bear the boat away to accelerate.
- Take the sea state into consideration when timing your acceleration. It will take longer to reach full speed in choppy conditions than in flat.
- Don't jump out on the trapeze until there is some flow over the centreboard or you will push the boat sideways.
- If the line is port bias your angle of attack to the line will be worse than on a starboard-bias line, so if queuing the same distance back you will need more time to accelerate on a port-bias line.

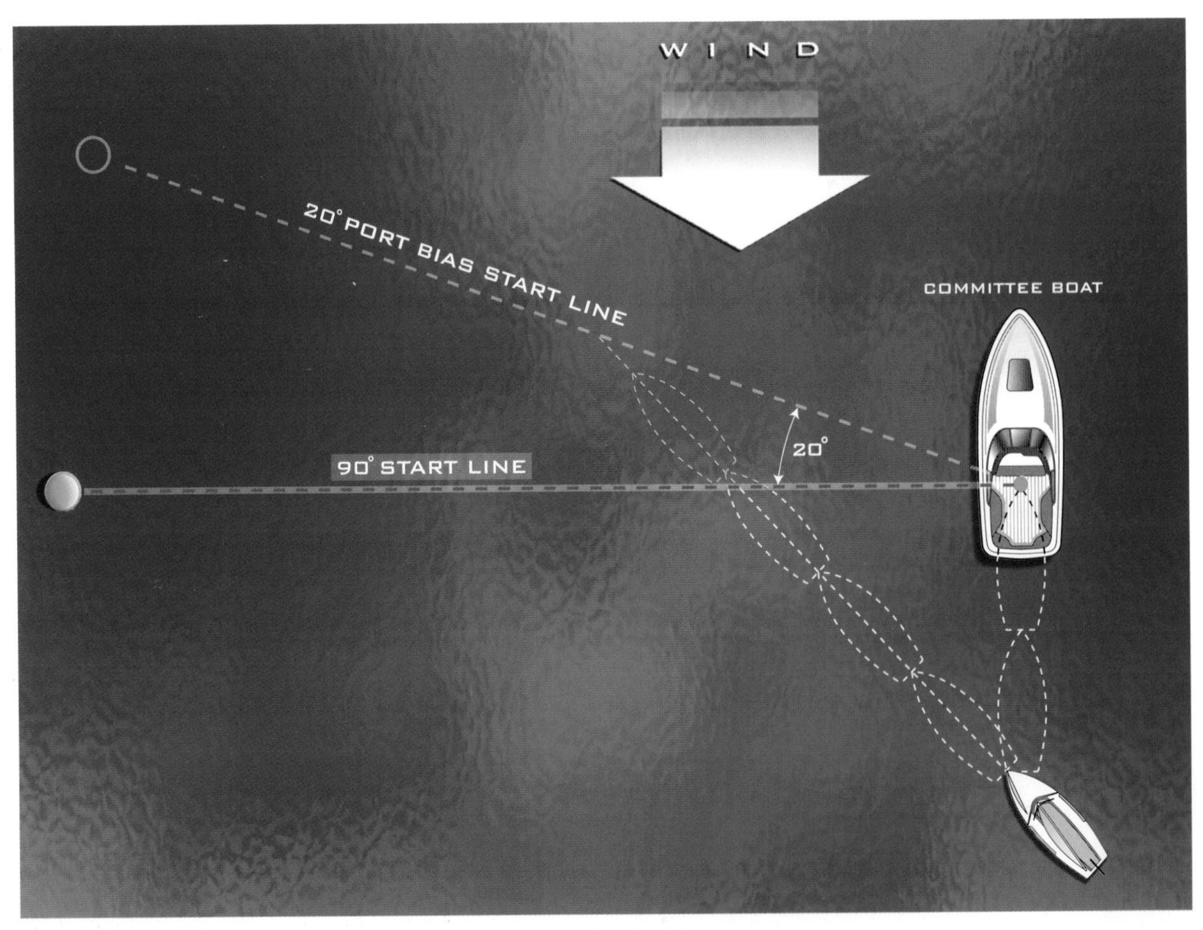


*The bias on the start line makes a big difference to your angle of attack. If you queue two boat lengths back on a 20 degree port bias line it will take over a boat length of extra sailing to cross over a square line, so be careful of late wind shifts!*

# Starting 14

# 15 Tactics and Strategy

## Observation and Prioritizing

Once you have good boat-handling and boat speed through a range of conditions, being successful at sailing will come down to good decision-making. The reason this is so difficult is that there are a huge number of variables to allow for, and no race is ever exactly the same as another. Experience makes a big difference to your tactical ability: the longer you race, the more situations you will come across and you will find out what works.

It is interesting that when most people lose a sailing race they know exactly why, it is rarely because of something they did not know about or understand, but more often something they just had not noticed. I believe there are two key words to remember when thinking about tactics pre-race: observation and prioritizing. You need to observe the variables for that particular day.

### Variables to Observe

- Wind (is it steady, oscillating, unstable, veering, backing etc?)
- Wind strength (which settings should you be on? How slow will it be to tack?)
- Weather forecast compared to conditions (do the current conditions match the forecast?)
- Tide or current (is there any current? Which way is it going? Is it the same strength across the course?)
- Sea state (is it flat, choppy or wavy?)
- Land (are you racing close enough to any land that it will affect the wind or tide?)
- Other boats (what is the size of the fleet?)
- Course (is the first beat true to the wind? How big is the course compared to the number of boats?)
- Start line (are there any transits? What is the bias? How long is the line?)

Once you have the answers to the questions these observations raise, you will be in a good position to identify the priorities for the race.

### Observations

- Light, steady sea breeze.
- No tide.
- Flat water.
- No nearby land.
- Large fleet of boats.
- Small course.
- Short start line, no bias, good transit.



## Priorities

- Must get a good start at all costs (with a steady wind and small course there will be little room for a comeback)!
- Start in space, probably in the middle of the line (no bias, so being clear is most important and, with a clear transit, starting in the middle will be quite easy and give the most options for a short beat).
- Keep clean wind at all times (with little differences in wind it will be most important to stay in clear lanes rather than go a certain way).
- Stay away from laylines (with a lot of boats and a short course the laylines could be very congested).
- Concentrate on technique and sail-settings and sail a high VMG (the high number of boats and small course will make the first beat very congested, so there will be tight lanes and it will be important to point high to stay in them.)

These priorities may look fairly simple but sticking to them would get you towards the front of most fleets.

## Roles and Responsibilities

In a two-man boat you will have to decide who is looking at the tactics and calling the tacks. In most classes the crew has the most time to look around, so is in a good position to call what is coming towards the boat in terms of gusts, lulls and other boats. The helm can then concentrate on the steering and look at the variables inside the boat, for example the compass and sail-settings. It might be that, in your class, it is the other way round and it is easier for the crew to have their head in the boat and for the helm to be looking outside. Either way I think it is a good idea to divide the jobs so that one of you is responsible for the information coming from outside the boat, and the other for the information inside the boat.

*It is normally the crews responsibility to call the upwind layline especially in strong winds.*

## Communication

Helm and crew need to keep their team-mate(s) closely informed on the information they are receiving so that there is a continual dialogue between you. When it comes to actually making the decisions during a race I think it needs to be one person's job, but that person does not have to be the same for each leg of the course. A lot of teams do discuss the options and make joint decisions but, with the courses being so short and there being so many variables to consider, it seems an inefficient way of doing things.

Below is a typical dialogue between a helm and crew similar to that of Nick and I in our 470, with the crew looking out of the boat upwind and the helm looking out downwind.

### UPWIND

**CREW:** *"We have got a gust about to hit in 50 metres."*

**HELM:** *"OK, when it hits I am going to ease the jib fairlead back, so don't worry about easing the sheet."*

**CREW:** *"3… 2… 1… gust hitting now. It has lifted us a bit there, but I don't think it's going to last very long, so sail the boat quite low and fast to try to get across some of the fleet before the header."*

**HELM:** *"I'll lift the centreboard a little then. Can you stand back, as I am struggling to get the boat planing."*

**CREW:** *"Once we get this header we are going to tack, and if the boats to leeward start tacking we'll make sure we tack before them rather than across."*

**HELM:** *"How many boats are on that side of us?"*

**CREW:** *"About 30 per cent of the fleet. The wind is beginning to head there, and the leeward boats are starting to tack. Ready to tack?"*

**HELM:** *"Ready."*

**CREW:** *"Let's tack."*

### DOWNWIND

**HELM:** *"There is a good gust on the other side of the run so we're going to look for a gybe quite soon."*

**CREW:** *"OK, it feels on the spinnaker as though we have been lifted."*

**HELM:** *"Let's go for a gybe, then."*

*(After gybe)*

**CREW:** *"It feels as though we can sail quite low on this gybe and still catch the waves."*

**HELM:** *"I'm going to hold some height for now. Once the gust hits us then we can go low with it. Gust just about to hit… hitting now… there's still more to come. Let's start sailing lower now."*

**CREW:** *"Right, let's get in sync with these waves."*

As you can see, the conversation is not only about what is about to come but also about what they will do once the shift, gust, lull or boat arrives ensuring that everything runs smoothly as the change happens.

# 15 Tactics and Strategy

# 15 Tactics and Strategy

# 15 Tactics and Strategy

## Compass

The compass is the most useful and valuable tool when tracking the wind during the race. There are many different opinions on how you should use a compass and in how much detail you should track the wind pre-start. It is important to remember that the more complicated you make your compass work, the more time it will take out of your pre-start and the more difficult it will be to use during the race. Here is a guide:

### Using a Compass

- Head upwind on starboard keeping a close eye on the compass for a minimum of five minutes.
- Once you have a good idea of your maximum lift, header and mean numbers, write them down.
- Tack onto port for another five minutes and write down the numbers for a lift, header and mean on this tack.
- When you are on your mean heading go head-to-wind and take a reading and write it down.
- Once you are back down at the start area, head up on starboard and check if you are lifted, mean or headed so that you are tracking the wind.
- Once you are in start sequence and you don't have enough time to sail on starboard, use your head-to-wind reading to see where the wind is relative to mean.

This process looks a lot more complicated and time-consuming than it actually is. There are other things you can be doing while getting your numbers. It will give you the opportunity to tune upwind and do a practice downwind and will only really concern the person responsible for the compass.

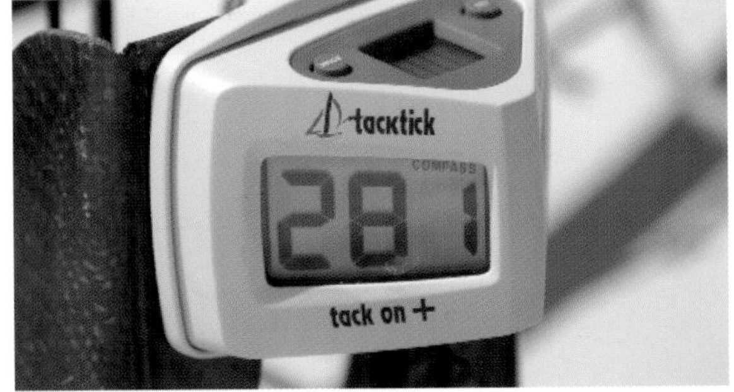


*Some classes are allowed digital compasses, these offer a higher level of accuracy but take fractionally longer to react to changes.*

## See Training Exercise 6

## Laylines

Calling the laylines is normally the crew's job. There is not really any special way of calling laylines accurately except by building up experience of your class's tacking angles in different wind and sea conditions. You will not always know exactly where the layline is, and if you are struggling to get it right you are probably trying to call them too early. Remember, you are leaving yourself tactically vulnerable by getting onto the layline too early: if the wind lifts you will be overstood and if the wind heads you will have little room to tack up, if you are not winning there is a strong chance of someone tacking in front of you and giving you dirty wind. When calling the layline, err on the side of caution to either overstand or understand, depending on the conditions. In lighter winds and flatter water you will do better to understand than overstand the layline, as doing a double tack if you cannot lay the mark will cost you little distance, but having to reach in could let a lot of boats in. When there are strong winds and big seas, however, a double tack can cost you a lot of distance but having to crack off will cost you very little.

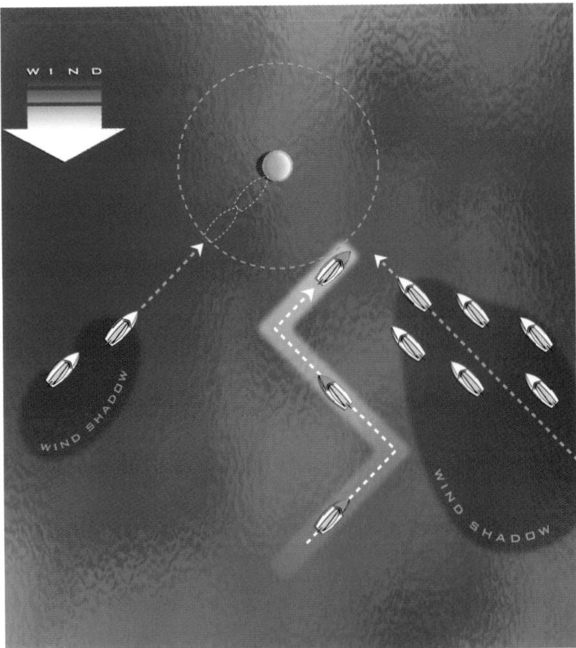


*When racing in a tight fleet, there is often more space and clean air in the centre of the course towards the top of the beat. Only go to the layline just prior to the 2 boat length circle so you can still tack into a tight lane.*

## See Training Exercise 8

## Covering

Sometimes when winning a race you will feel a need to cover the boat behind; to give them dirty wind and make sure they don't get a favourable gust or wind shift that you don't. A good technique, if you want to cover but are concerned about getting locked into a tacking duel, is to push the boat behind out onto a side. This works especially well if there is a side of the course you believe will pay or if there is more of one tack to do than the other. To do this you put a tight cover on the boat behind whenever they are on the tack taking them away from the side you are trying to push them to. When they tack onto the tack towards the layline, leave them with a little bit of room so they are tempted to hold for longer. Once you get them out onto the layline you can tack on them and they have nowhere left to go and have to either overstand or stay in dirty wind. This technique works much better in steady winds than in shifty, gusty winds. When the wind is shifty and gusty it is better to sail your own race by tacking as the headers hit you: it will force the boat behind to either tack in your dirty wind or stay on the headed tack.

If you are the boat being covered, tack away immediately when the boat in front tacks on you. This will give them no chance to settle and they will struggle to tack immediately back. If they do manage to get into a covering position on you, try to stay centrally on the course away from the laylines and, if all else fails, make sure you cover the boat behind. Have the attitude that, while you are sailing upwind, the ball is in their court and that you are just trying to limit the damage so that when you get on the downwind it will be you who makes the moves and does the covering.

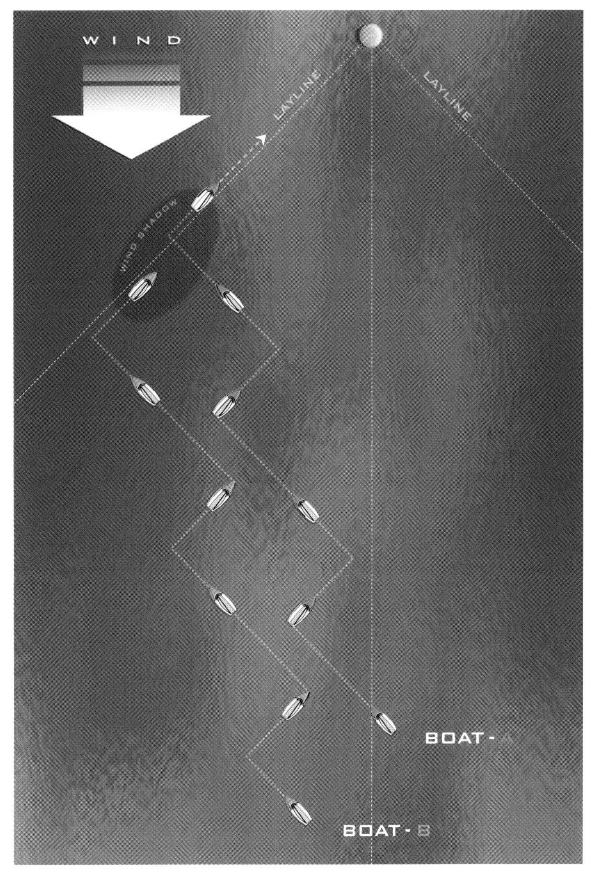


*Pushing a boat to a layline can be a good way to cover especially if there is a side you want them to go to. Here boat A only tacks on B whilst on port tack allowing a small amount of room whilst on starboard to push them towards the port layline.*

## Recovering from a Bad Start

The ability to recover from a bad start is an essential skill if you are to do well over an event. In most events in which I have competed we have made a mistake at the beginning of a race that has left us with a lot of catching up to do: in these situations it is easy to lose perspective on the points and give up. Remember, moving from 30th to 27th is a bigger gain than from 3rd to 1st, even if it does not often feel like it is. Here are some tips for when things have started badly:

- Put the mistake behind you and be positive.
- Concentrate on catching up with the boats just in front rather than looking for one big lucky gain.
- Often there is more space at the top of the first beat in the middle rather than on the sides.
- If you are reaching first try to avoid a luffing match, or the leading group will pull away further, as they are sailing a more direct route to the mark.
- Be aggressive on the running legs. The first run is probably your best chance to get back in touch with the front group. Stay away from congested groups of boats and concentrate on sailing a fast VMG at all times.
- On subsequent beats, work really hard to always remain on the lifted tacks. It will be hard to find lanes because of the boats ahead, so a lot of the boats around you will mindlessly sail out to corners, giving you the opportunity to overtake.

49er
GBR2
49er
885
39
US
49er
GBR
USA
NAUTICA
ROLEX
ROLEX

49er.org
POL 16
AUT251
ITA3
POL 36
LAYLINE
SPRENGER

# 16 Event Preparation

In sailing the way you go about preparing for an event will make a huge difference to your chances of success. One of the main reasons for this is that no two events are exactly the same: the number and standard of competitors will vary, as will the weather. Add this to the many equipment variables and there is a lot to consider before the event begins, if you are going to give yourself a chance of fulfilling your potential.

## Calibrate Your Settings

Far too many sailors check their settings at the beginning of the season and then simply leave them over the year. They are likely, however, to change as the rigging stretches and the spreaders and mast foot bed in. For this reason it is a must to check them at the beginning of each event, especially if you have de-rigged and travelled to get there. Ideally you should check them each day so that you have confidence in them whenever you go to the water.

## Pre-Event Training

It is important to stop trying new ideas during your last few training sessions before a big event, and concentrate on making sure you have good boat-handling and are race-sharp. Trying new things can be distracting and should be done away from any performance regattas. In your last few training sessions, go back to basics, doing boat-handling exercises and taking part in some small races.

There is always a temptation, when doing your final build-up to an important event, to over-train, and a compromise needs to be found between getting a good number of hours on the water so that you feel prepared and practised and doing so much that you feel stale. Prior to a week-long event, try to think how you will feel towards the end of the week rather than at the beginning: if you think you might feeling tired, take a day off before it starts.

## Equipment Preparation

Racing sailors and their boats compete in a huge number of races; events are often lost due to gear failure. It is absolutely vital to do a detailed check before the event starts. A good idea is to split the jobs between the helm and the crew. If you are well-organized enough to do it, writing up a checklist guarantees that you don't miss anything out. When you do your check is important: it is no use checking something that will take a few days to order or fix the day before the event. No matter how good your checks are, inevitably sometimes, through no fault of your own, things will break or fail to work. For this reason a spare kit-bag needs to be prepared. What you put in a spare kit-bag depends on whether you can take it out on the water and where you can store it. If you have your own coach on a RIB you will be able to keep quite a lot of kit on the coach boat, which will resolve most problems. However most people don't have a coach and will want to put a small bag on a rescue boat, and you will have to choose the most important spares to have in that bag. This will vary according to the class. The longer you sail a class the more you will know which parts of the boat are vulnerable to breakdowns. The list will act as a good starting point for most classes.

### Basic Spare Kit-bag

- Countdown timer
- Main, jib and spinnaker sheets cut to the right length
- Length of 3mm rope
- Multi-tool
- Pliers
- Duct tape
- Insulation tape
- Spinnaker repair tape
- Whipping twine and needle
- Tiller extension with universal joint
- Trapeze harness (if sailing a trapeze boat)
- Mainsail batten
- Spare hi-load block
- Spare auto ratchet

# 16 Event Preparation

## Local Knowledge

Every venue has different sailing conditions, so there is often a large gain to be made by gathering information about the venue prior to the event. The best way to do this is to sail at the venue yourself and keep notes on the weather you sailed in and any traits you noticed. It is well worth getting hold of a chart of your racecourse as well as the tide times. This will give you good factual information which will give you an advantage. A good idea is to laminate these and keep them on your boat. Gaining knowledge from other sailors' personal experiences of the venue can be risky. Make sure the information is coming from someone you respect for both their ability and reliability and check that they were sailing a boat with similar characteristics to yours. It is easy to fall into the trap of listening to lots of local advice then putting the blinkers on while racing – it seems wherever you sail, the line 'It's never normally like this' comes out. Sometimes it is best just to go with what you know and see and use only the factual information.

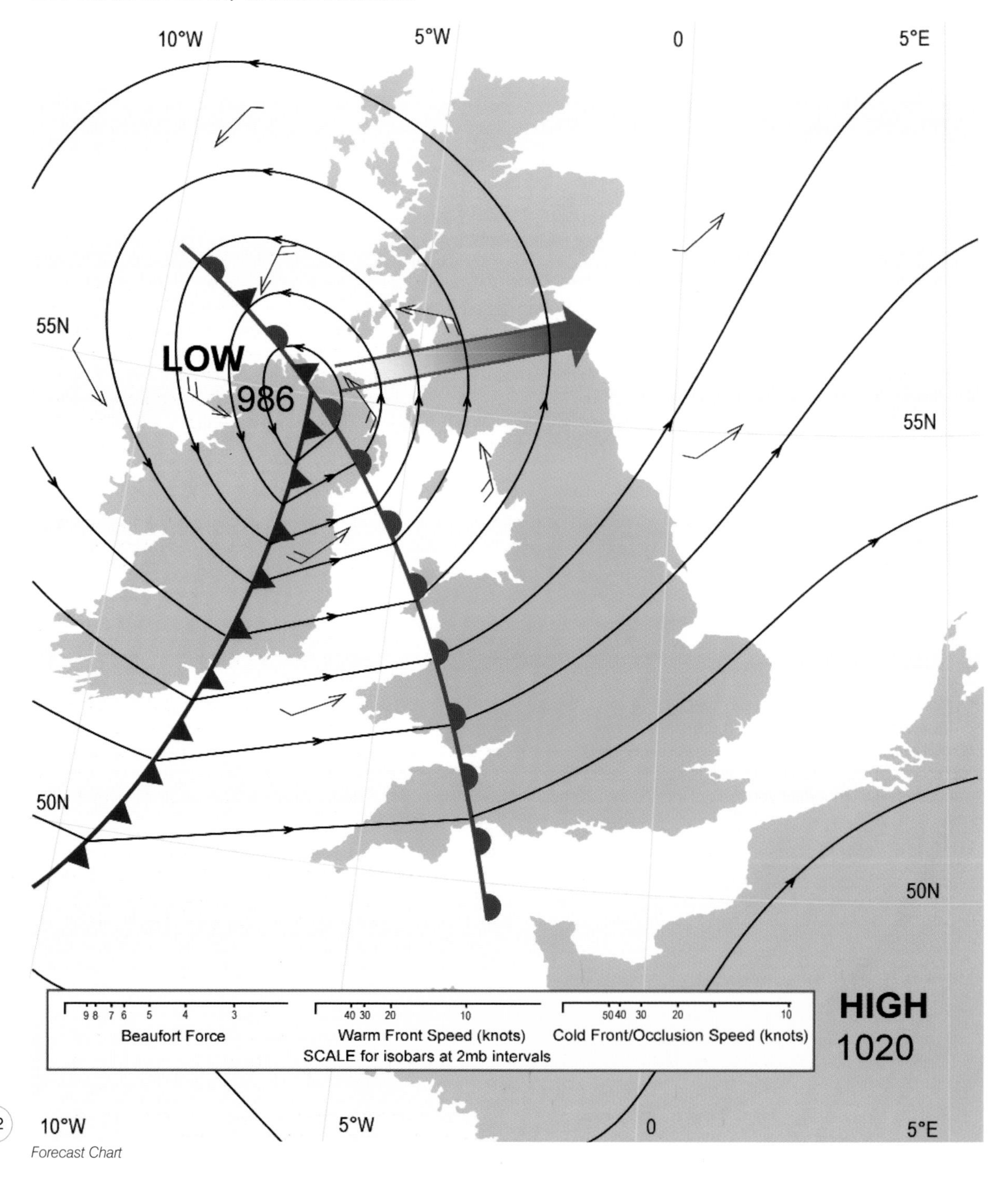




*Forecast Chart*

## Mental Preparation

Hopefully, by being prepared for all the different aspects of the sport you will go into the event feeling confident, focused and ready to race. Sailing is all about observations and decision-making, so your mental preparation is the most important factor. In the final build-up towards an important event. Try to be as single-minded as possible. Don't look at what your competitors are doing or how they are preparing, just keep focused on what you need to do to achieve your performance goal. If you are feeling nervous, try to forget about your goal and just concentrate on the processes that are important for that day. Often at Olympic events you see a lot of people walking around with earphones on, listening to music. This is quite a good way to shut yourself off from the rest of the world; focus and concentrate on the things you need to do. Looking at the results in the evening can be distracting, as it makes you think about your goal again, rather than the processes. It also makes you very aware of where your rivals are in relation to you, and in sailing there are enough variables to think about without considering the ones you can't control.

Remember, different conditions will require different states of mind: in light winds you have plenty of time to make decisions but you have to be more precise and your movements around the boat need to be smooth, so make sure when you launch you are feeling calm and focused (like a snooker player); in stronger winds your decision-making will need to be faster and you will have to feel more energetic and alert, so it can be worth winding yourself up a bit (more like a boxer would).

## Physical Preparation

Assuming that you have done the correct physical training for your class, the main thing when at an event is to take action to avoid injury or fatigue. Eating and drinking the right things is a key issue for sailors. Long hours on the water make it difficult to get enough in at the right time, and depleting energy levels will make a big difference over the course of an event. It is well worth buying a good hydration drink; the powder form is the easiest to carry around and you can mix it up when you need it. Energy bars and high-carbohydrate snack-type foods are also good for between meals and on the water. You will have to shop around a bit, as some are fairly tasteless and difficult to eat. Evening meals should be high in carbohydrate, but also balanced, as it is important you are getting the Recommended Daily Allowance of all your vitamins and minerals to avoid illness.

One of the key problems for racing sailors is when they don't have a coach or rescue boat to store their lunch and don't want to carry too much on board and weigh the boat down. Although I can fully understand this problem fluid and snacks do need to be carried in order to be race-sharp over a full day, especially if there are strong winds or it is hot. You can reduce the storage problem significantly by having a drink and snack immediately before launching and one ready for when you are back on shore.

## Team Event Attitude

When you start sailing at events the tension and stress for both the helm and crew is likely to be greater than when you are in training. It is essential that you both really pull together and work as a team, both on and off the water. It is likely, over the course of a week's racing, that you will have good and bad days, and you need to keep each other emotionally stable through these and make sure your confidence as individuals remains high.

Remember, different people like to prepare in different ways. Just because you are a team does not mean you should have the same bedtimes and pre-race habits. Most good teams will have the attitude, when it comes to the racing, that we win together, we lose together, and we will never give up.

# 17 Training Exercise 1

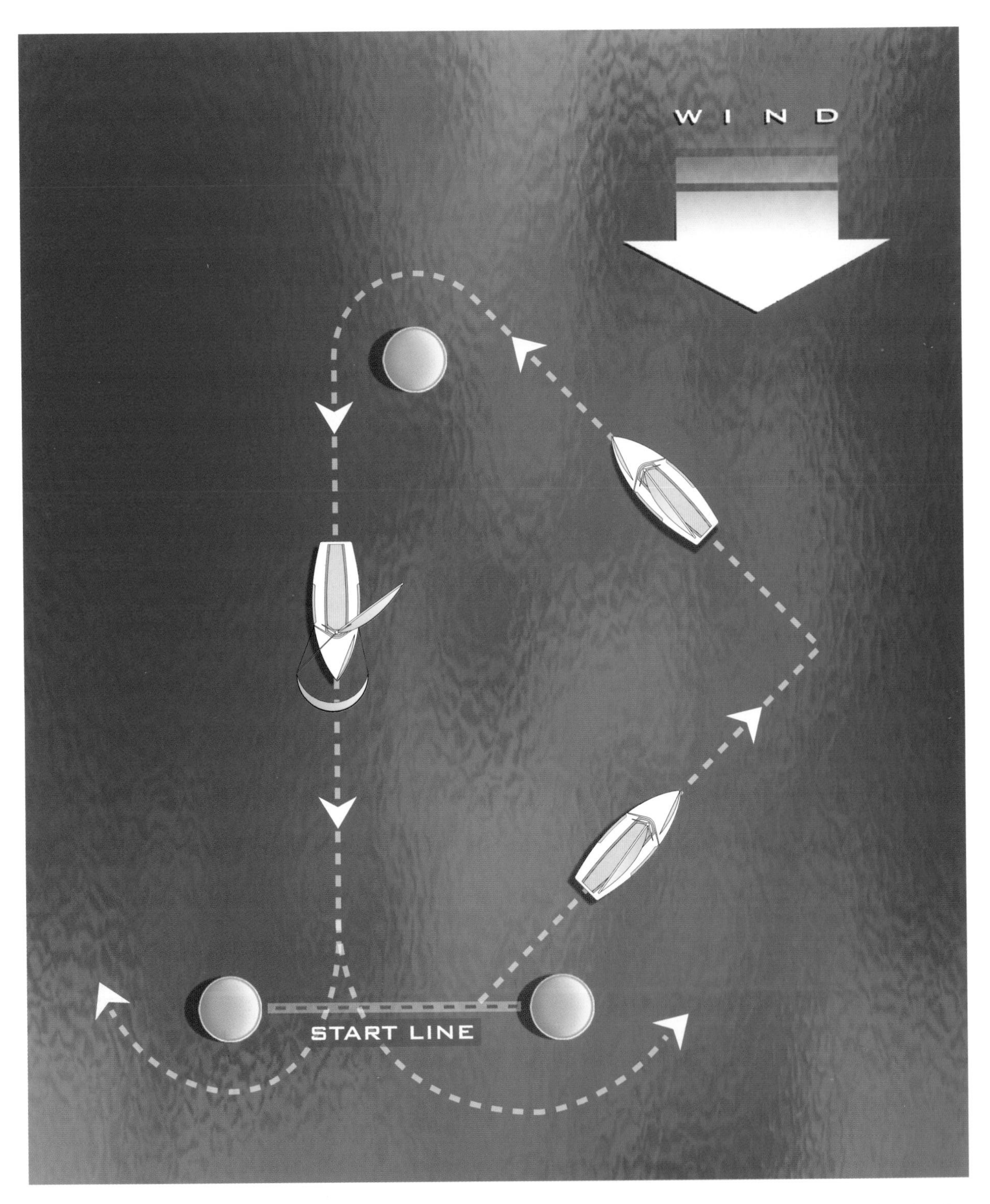


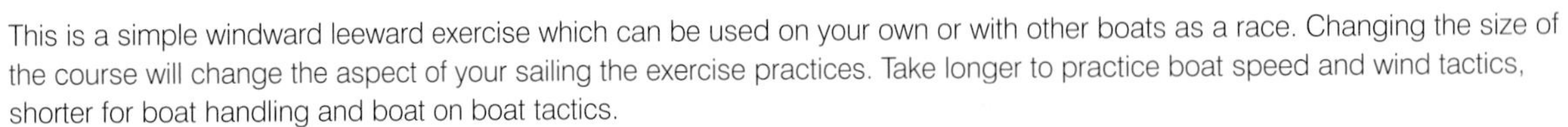
This is a simple windward leeward exercise which can be used on your own or with other boats as a race. Changing the size of the course will change the aspect of your sailing the exercise practices. Take longer to practice boat speed and wind tactics, shorter for boat handling and boat on boat tactics.

# Training Exercise 2 17

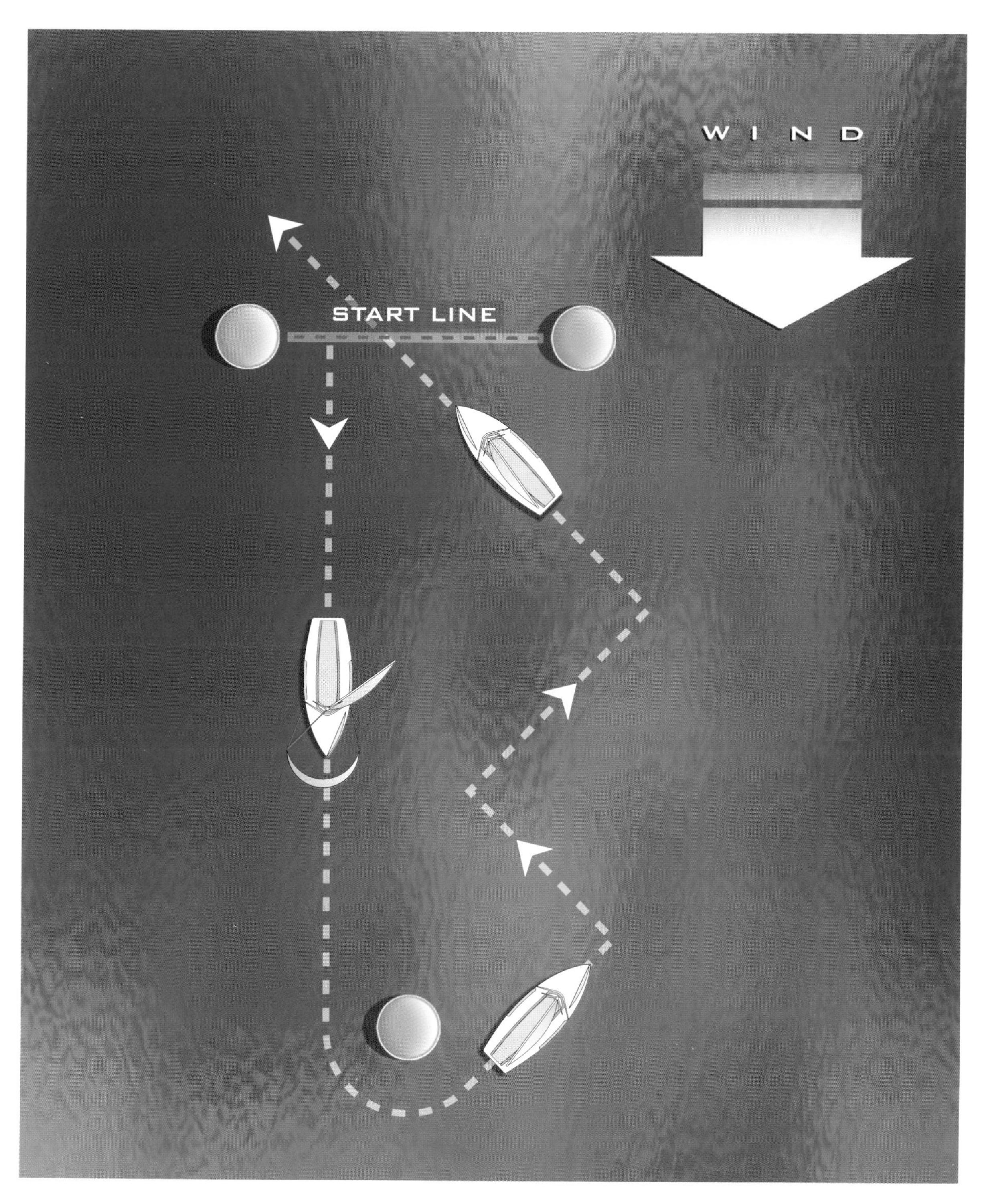


This reverse windward - leeward puts more emphasis on the downwind sailing as you and the boats you are sailing against are not spread out as you might be after a beat, it usually means a congested leeward mark and a tight beat replicating the 2nd beat of larger race. It usually best to set a rule that everyone must be on starboard with spinnakers down at start time.

# 17 Training Exercise 3

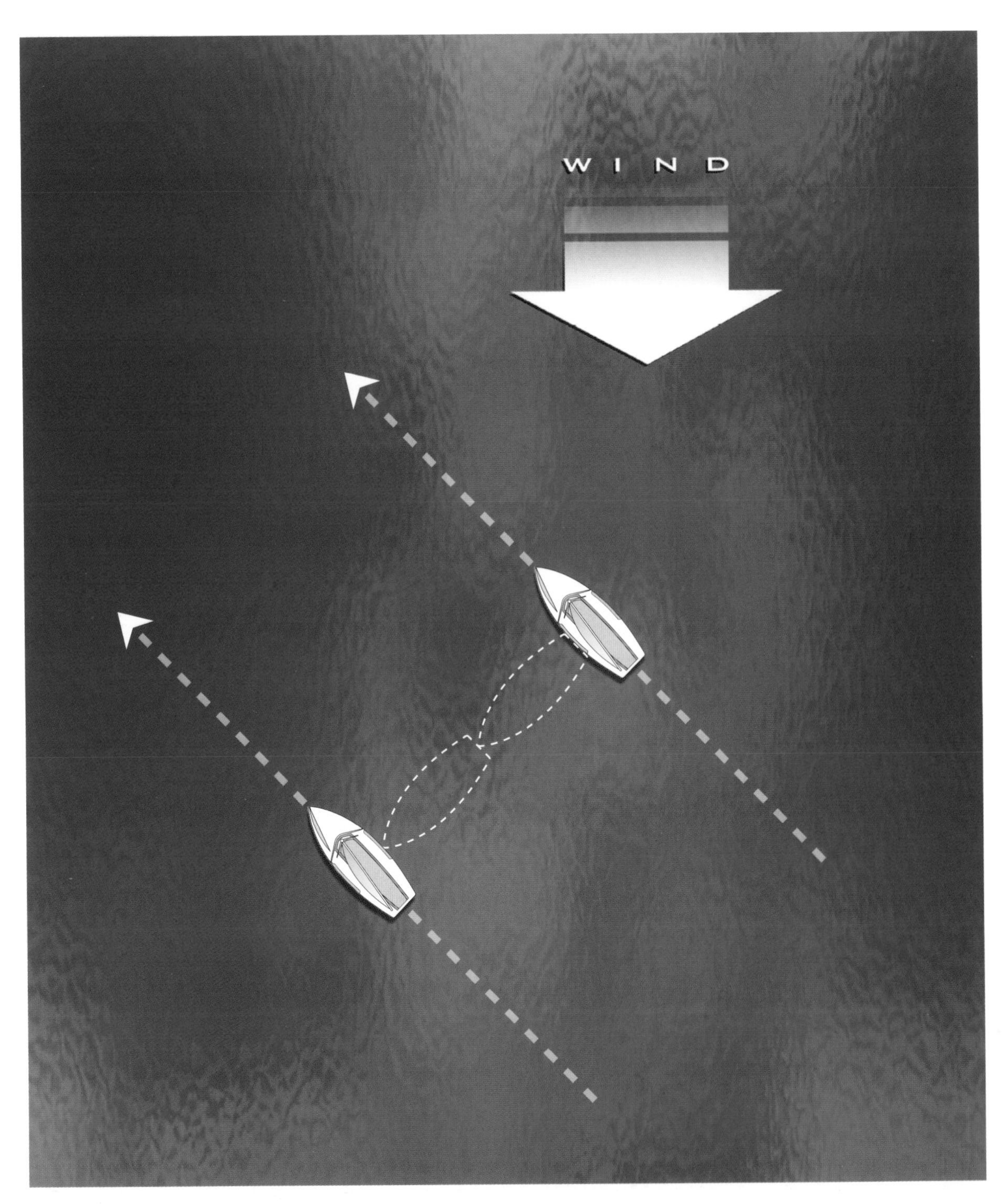


Upwind boat tuning is used to practice and test technique, settings and equipment. The success of tuning largely depends on how the boats line up at the beginning. Make sure you are not effecting each others wind, then concentrate on sailing your fastest VMG not trying to muck up each other. Keep track of wind shifts using a compass and try and finish the tuning run when you are on the same compass number as when you started.

# Training Exercise 4 **17**

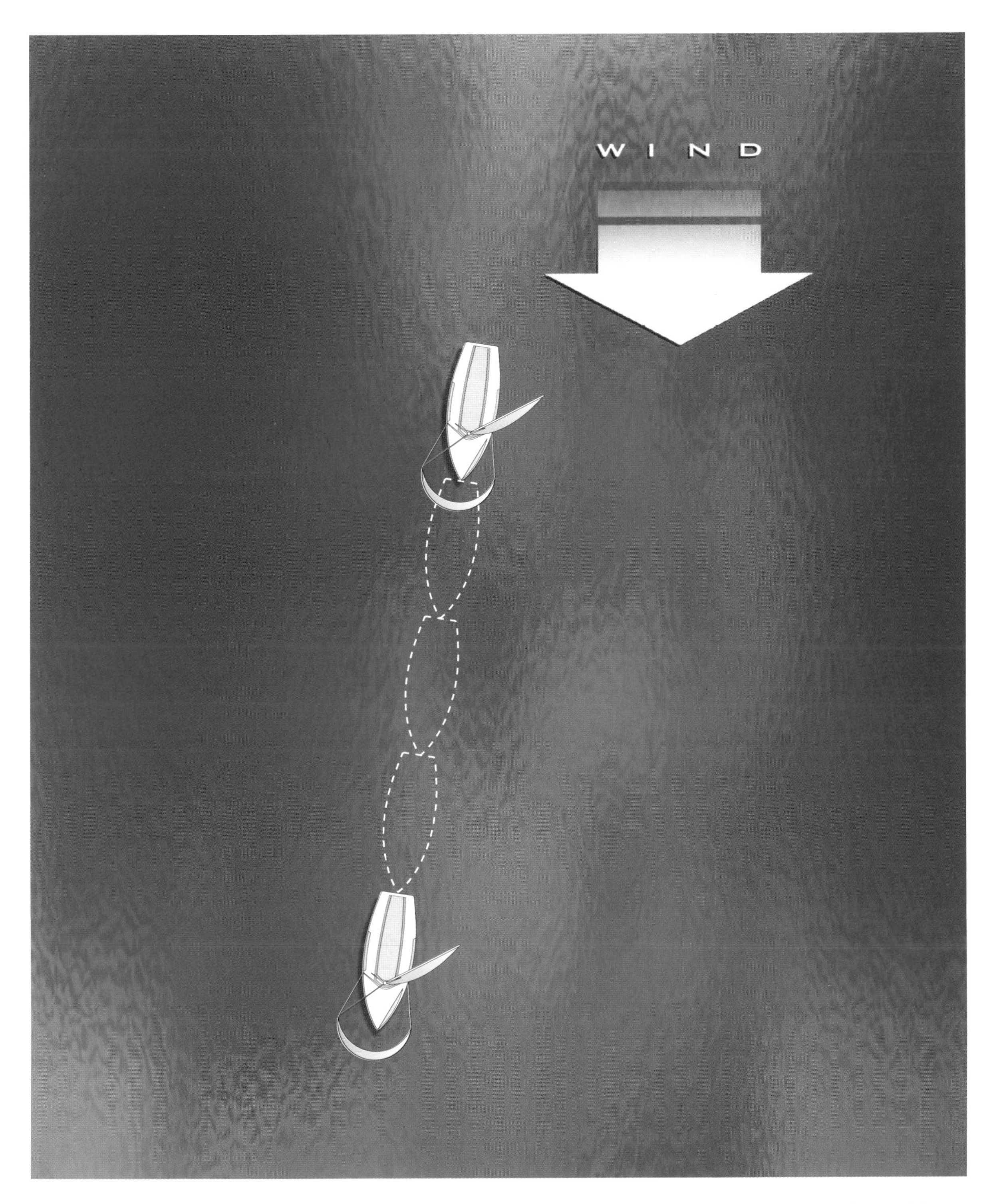


Downwind boat tuning really needs to be done to a mark even if it is a very long way away, the boats should start in a straight line behind each other and make sure that the boat in front is not having its wind effected. Whilst sailing downwind stay reasonably close together but don't gybe on each others wind.

# 17 Training Exercise 5

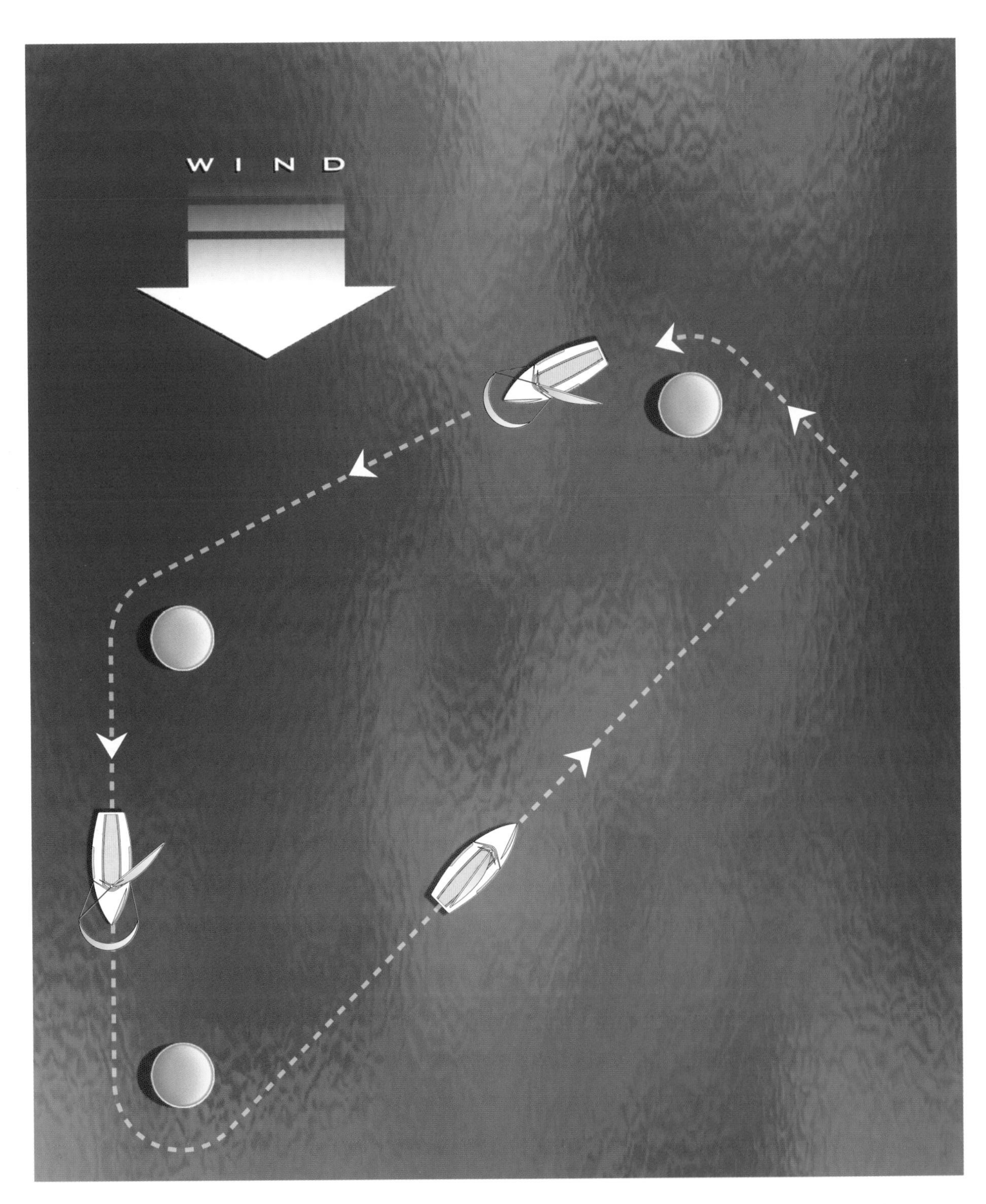


This exercises practices hoisting to a reach, reaching, rounding a wing mark and running. It replicates the downwind of an outer loop trapezoid course, if you are doing it with other boats do a gate start with the gate boat coming across on starboard and tacking to windward of the other boats.

# Training Exercise 6 17

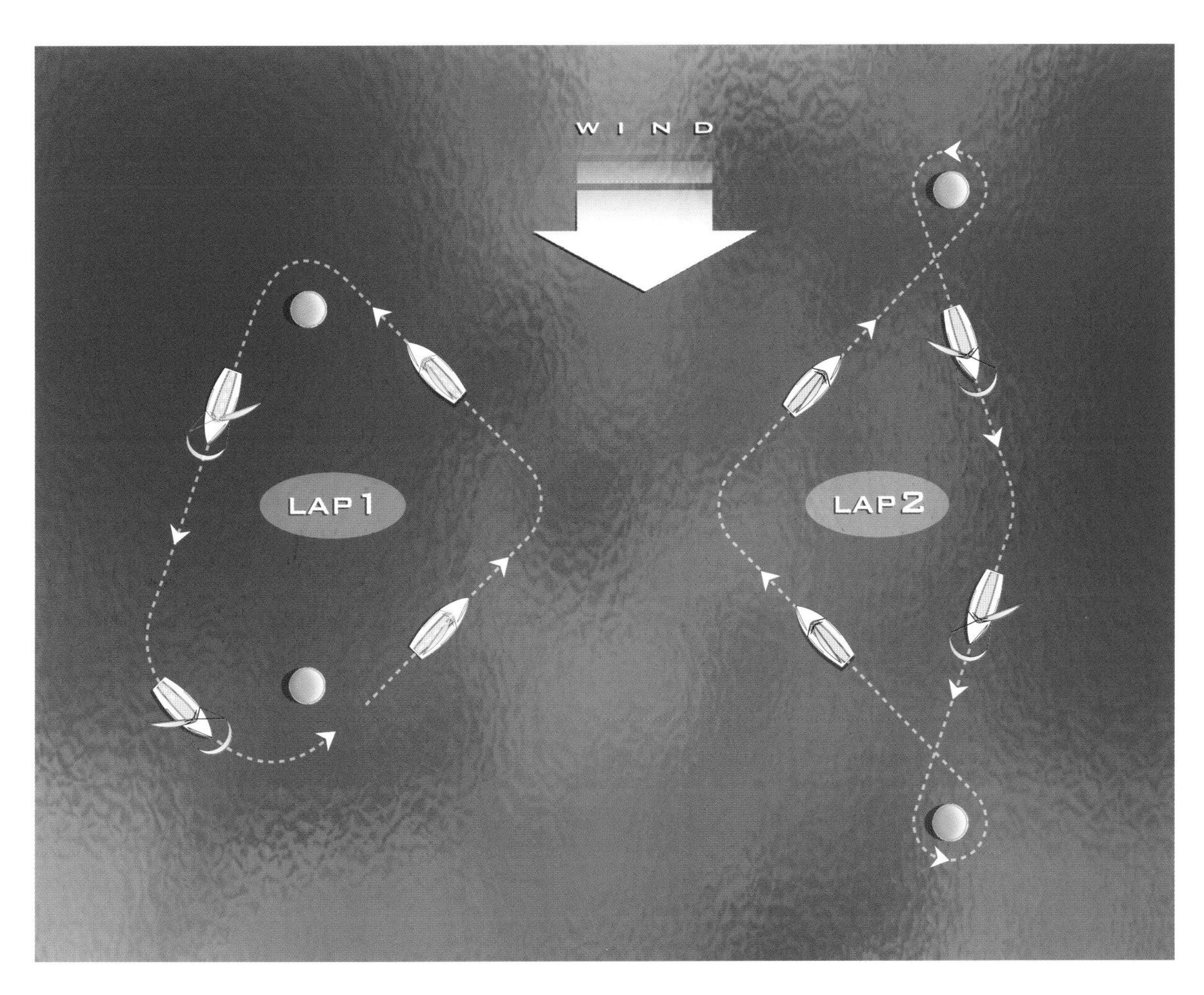


A boat handling course that practices most manouveres from a race. First lap sail to the starboard layline doing a straight hoist at windward mark, gybe, then drop at leeward mark. Second lap, tack after leeward mark got to the port layline, gybe hoist at windward mark and drop gybe at leeward mark. Make the course comfortable to start with then shorter as you get better.

# 17 Training Exercise 7

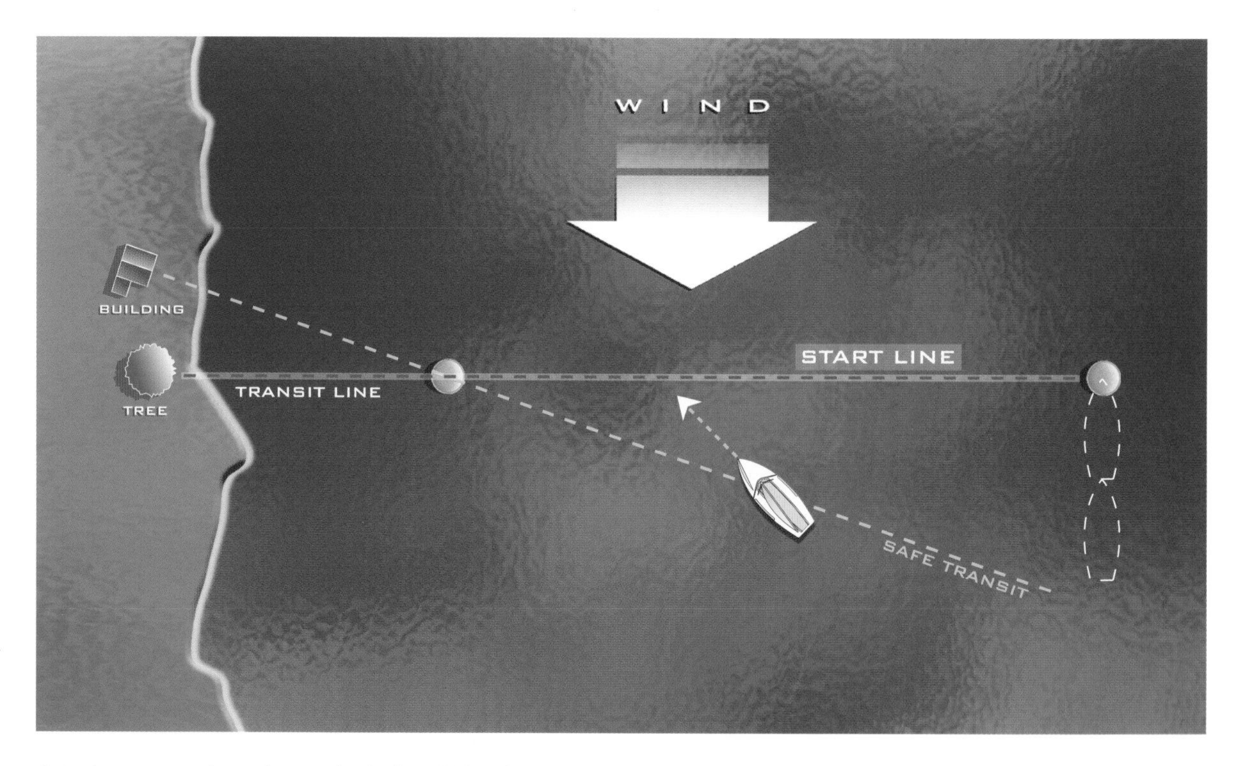


Set a long start and practice starting in the middle of the line, if possible get a coach to look down the line and tell you afterwards how far or close you were to being on it. Try some with no transit and some with transit and safe transit.

# Training Exercise 8 **17**

8. This is a simple tacking exercise that can be carried out a number of ways. One way is to line up together and do it on a whistle, another way is for one boat to start ahead and cover the other boat, however you do it, it is good to do next to another boat so you have a benchmark and to put yourself under some pressure.

WWW.VOLVOCARS.CO.UK/SAILING

'Sailing is definitely one of those sports when just as you think you are getting somewhere you do something stupid, here we are in one of our numerous capsizes throughout the photo shoot, have fun!'
Joe Glanfield
for life

# Notes

# Notes

# Index

# Index

# Index

# RYA Membership

Promoting and Protecting Boating

www.rya.org.uk

**1 Important** To help us comply with Data Protection legislation, please tick ***either*** Box A or Box B (you must tick Box A to ensure you receive the full benefits of RYA membership). The RYA will not pass your data to third parties.

☐ **A.** I wish to join the RYA and receive future information on member services, benefits (as listed in RYA Magazine and website) and offers.

☐ **B.** I wish to join the RYA but do not wish to receive future information on member services, benefits (as listed in RYA Magazine and website) and offers.

**When completed, please send this form to: RYA, RYA House, Ensign Way, Hamble, Southampton, SO31 4YA**

**2**

| | Title | Forename | Surname | Date of Birth | Male | Female |
|---|---|---|---|---|---|---|
| 1. | | | | DD / MM / YY | | |
| 2. | | | | DD / MM / YY | | |
| 3. | | | | DD / MM / YY | | |
| 4. | | | | DD / MM / YY | | |

**Address**

**Town** **County** **Post Code**

**Evening Telephone** **Daytime Telephone**

**email** **Signature:** __________ **Date:** __________

## 3 Type of membership required: *(Tick Box)*

☐ ***Personal*** *Annual rate £37 or £34 by Direct Debit*

☐ ***Under 21*** *Annual rate £12 (no reduction for Direct Debit)*

☐ ***Family**** *Annual rate £56 or £52 by Direct Debit*

** Family Membership: 2 adults plus any under 21s all living at the same address*

**4** Please tick ONE box to show your main boating interest.

- ☐ Yacht Racing
- ☐ Dinghy Racing
- ☐ Personal Watercraft
- ☐ Powerboat Racing
- ☐ Motor Boating
- ☐ Yacht Cruising
- ☐ Dinghy Cruising
- ☐ Inland Waterways
- ☐ Windsurfing
- ☐ Sportsboats and RIBs

Please see Direct Debit form overleaf

## Instructions to your Bank or Building Society to pay by Direct Debit

Please complete this form and return it to:
Royal Yachting Association, RYA House, Ensign Way, Hamble, Southampton, Hampshire SO31 4YA

DIRECT Debit

To The Manager: Bank/Building Society

Address:

Post Code:

**2. Name(s) of account holder(s)**

**3. Branch Sort Code**

| | | — | | | — | | |
|---|---|---|---|---|---|---|---|

**4. Bank or Building Society account number**

| | | | | | | | |
|---|---|---|---|---|---|---|---|

**Originators Identification Number**

| 9 | 5 | 5 | 2 | 1 | 3 |
|---|---|---|---|---|---|

**5. RYA Membership Number (For office use only)**

**6. Instruction to pay your Bank or Building Society**
Please pay Royal Yachting Association Direct Debits from the account detailed in this instruction subject to the safeguards assured by The Direct Debit Guarantee.
I understand that this instruction may remain with the Royal Yachting Association and, if so, details will be passed electronically to my Bank/Building Society.

Signature(s) ____________________

Date ____________________

**Banks and Building Societies may not accept Direct Debit instructions for some types of account**

**Cash, Cheque, Postal Order enclosed** £
Made payable to the Royal Yachting Association

**077**

**Office use only:** Membership Number Allocated

**Office use / Centre Stamp**